When the Impossible Happens

When the Impossible Happens

Bizarre events that defy science from levitation to spontaneous human combustion

Editor: Peter Brookesmith

BLACK CAT

Acknowledgements

Photographs were supplied by Aerofilms, Aldus Books, Associated Press, Bodleian Picture Library, British Library, Richard Burgess, Jean-Loup Charmet, Bruce Coleman, Colorific, Contrad Research Library, Culver Pictures, Dowson & Mason Ltd., Mary Evans Picture Library, George Feifer, Joel Finler Collection, Werner Forman Archive, Fortean Picture Library, John Frost, Glaister & Rentoul, Mack Goethe, Nancy Heinl, Michael Holford Library, Robert Hunt Picture Library, Hutchinson Publishing Group, ILN, Illinois State Historical Library, Keystone, Kobal Collection, Brian Larkman, Leicester Mercury, University of Leeds, William MacQuitty, Ross McWhirter, City of Manchester Art Galleries, Gregor Mendel Institute, NASA/Science Photo Library, National Portrait Gallery, Novosti, Photri, Popperfoto, Press Agency (New York) Ltd., Press Association, Psychic News, Reeves Pictures, Rex Features, Scala, Scottish Daily Herald & Sunday Mail, Ronald Sheridan Photo Library, Paul Sieveking, Sovfoto, Sun Newspaper, Syndication International, Daily Telegraph Colour Library, UPI, White House Historical Association, David Williamson, World Government of the Age of Enlightenment, Yorkshire Evening Post, ZEFA.

Consultants to
The Unexplained
Professor A. J. Ellison
Dr J. Allen Hynek
Brian Inglis
Colin Wilson
Editorial Director
Brian Innes
Editor
Peter Brookesmith
Deputy Editor
Lynn Picknett
Executive Editor
Lesley Riley
Sub Editors
Mitzi Bales
Chris Cooper
Jenny Dawson
Hildi Hawkins

Picture Researchers
Anne Horton
Paul Snelgrove
Frances Vargo
Editorial Manager
Clare Byatt
Art Editor
Stephen Westcott
Designer
Richard Burgess
Art Buyer
Jean Hardy
Production Co-ordinator
Nicky Bowden
Volume Editor
Lorrie Mack
Assistants
Ruth Turner
Sarah Reason

Material in this publication previously appeared in the weekly partwork *The Unexplained*, © 1980-83

This edition copyright © 1984 Orbis Publishing Ltd
copyright © 1988 Macdonald & Co (Publishers) Ltd

First published 1984 by Orbis Publishing Ltd
Reprinted 1988 by Macdonald & Co (Publishers) Ltd under the Black Cat imprint

Macdonald & Co (Publishers) Ltd
3rd Floor, Greater London House
Hampstead Road, London NW1 7QX

a member of Maxwell Pergamon Publishing Corporation plc

ISBN 0-7481-0145-4

Printed in Belgium

Contents

Introduction

THERE WAS A TIME when people who witnessed unlikely events or who held unorthodox opinions ran the risk of torture or death at the hands of the Church. In later centuries the danger of meeting an unpleasant end for failing to conform in this way has receded; the poet and painter William Blake was merely given a sound thrashing by his father for saying he had seen some angels sitting in a tree, for instance. But that was in the 18th century, when a spirit of tolerance was deemed a natural outcome of taking a logical and rational view of the world. It was, however, tolerance that went only so far, as the youthful poet's tingling skin doubtless reminded him.

The guardians of truth today are not priests but scientists, and their weapons are not the thumbscrew and the rack (though one sometimes wonders if they did not wish it otherwise) but silence, derision, wilful ignorance and sometimes outright abuse. The intrepid researcher into the bizarre and anomalous risks all of these should he so much as whisper his interest to one of our white-coated witch doctors. For to science such events as spontaneous human combustion, levitation, impossible explosions and unnatural coincidences *can't happen*. They don't fit the rules that science recognises; there is no *known* means by which fish can flop to earth out of a clear sky – and for many scientists, what is not known is simply not possible – it just does not happen.

But such things, apparently, do happen. Furthermore, the unknown and unexpected persist in happening in science itself, much to the dismay of those rash enough to have said otherwise. Meteors and ball lightning are famous cases of phenomena long rejected by science as impossible. Greater embarrassment can be induced by various unkind reminders of the prophecies of scientists: Sir Ernest Rutherford, who first discovered how to split the atom, was convinced that the energy produced by doing so would be 'a very poor kind of thing' – a prediction for which the people of Hiroshima were, in due course of time, properly grateful. Simon Newcomb, a celebrated astronomer, declared the aeroplane 'utterly impossible' in 1902. Thomas J. Watson of IBM, no less, once calculated that there would be a world market for 'about five computers'. And so it goes on.

To anyone with an open mind, it is surely obvious that the 'impossible' happens all the time, which is another way of saying that science can examine and account for only a part – if a large and important part – of what we recognise as reality. So it is that science is sensibly silent about some of the wonders that we all take – perhaps too easily – for granted: the creative force that produces a great painting, a poem or a magnificently moving piece of music, the spirit that moves men to be heroes or the worst of villains, the enormous power of our feelings when we fall in love. Such things don't fit into the materialistic, predictable scheme of things that science can handle. There *are* those biologists and behaviourists who insist that consciousness – thought and feeling – is only an illusion produced by the brain's electrical activity and that 'ideas don't move muscles', but that is of a different order from the incapacity to accept that even the most seemingly obvious of rules can be broken.

It is matters such as these that are dealt with in this book. By their very nature they are almost impossible for science to investigate adequately; you cannot examine an event like spontaneous human combustion since it is impossible to reproduce it in the laboratory. And the great collector of reports of such peculiar occurrences, Charles Fort, may have put his finger on the key to the mystery with his notion of a 'cosmic joker' at work in the Universe.

After all, if we can play pranks upon one another, why shouldn't the Universe, of which we are but a part, laugh at itself from time to time? And, like a good magician, refuse to tell how the trick is done?

The cosmic joker will, therefore, play most merrily with reality – and with our all-too-human tendency to expect consistency in the world. He will on one occasion appeal to our own sense of humour – causing a truck laden with carrots to collide with another carrying olive oil to make the biggest carrot salad in the world, for instance, or inexorably drawing a man called Phang into a career in dentistry. He will, on the other hand, mock the scepticism of science by dropping an enormous lump of ice out of a blue sky to land at the feet of a distinguished meteorologist, forcing him to accept the unexplicable. No less outrageously, the cosmic joker presents sea monsters and UFOs to photographers, and then causes their cameras to jam for the first and last time.

But the jokes may be more subtle than that. What, for example, is one to make of the notorious photographs of fairies taken at Cottingley, England, earlier this century? Many critics have remarked how like scissors-and-paste jobs they look. Others may feel that such a trick is typical of the cosmic joker, who would, of course, make absolutely certain that the best evidence for such other-dimensional beings *should* seem so suspect. That is all part of the prank of tantalising innocent humans with a glimpse of such creatures in the first place. And if humanity insists on taking itself and its ideas so seriously, doesn't it *deserve* to be teased?

Welcome, then, to the games that reality can play.

PETER BROOKESMITH

Charles Fort

A wild talent

Stones that fall from the sky . . . strange lights in the heavens . . . plagues of butterflies . . . these and other anomalous phenomena obsessed researcher Charles Hoy Fort in the early 20th century. BOB RICKARD assesses Fort's continuing significance

UNKNOWN IN HIS OWN DAY, Charles Hoy Fort was rediscovered in 1947 to become a recognised – and revered – master of the study of strange phenomena and UFOs. His timid and withdrawn personality hid a bold and original mind, which he bent towards postulating solutions to the Earth's mysteries.

According to his biographer Damon Knight, Fort 'was built like a walrus. . . an utterly peaccable and sedentary man. He lived quietly with his wife, almost never went out or had visitors. . . spent the mornings working at home, afternoons in the library. . . .' Yet this unlikely character had a vivid imagination that was caught by every aspect of the anomalous, the bizarre, the occult and the unexplained that fascinates so many today. Because of his pioneering methods and wide range of interests, the word 'Fortean' is used to describe the study of strange phenomena.

A brief selection from Fort's writings might include: the appearance of people from nowhere and the disappearance of people into nowhere; spontaneous human combustion; unidentified flying objects; discoveries of America before Columbus; lights on the Moon; stigmatic wounds; rains of stones, blood, manna or animals from the skies; people with paranormal abilities; wolf children and wild men; teleportations and flights of objects; visions, levitations and other alleged miracles.

Fort was born in 1874 in Albany, New York, USA, to a fairly prosperous family of Dutch immigrants. Throughout his not too

In his quest for stories of anomalous phenomena, Charles Fort (previous page) spent several years in the 1920s among the archives of the British Library (right) at the British Museum in London. During his 'London period' he lived in Marchmont Street (previous page), then a run-down area, close to the British Museum. He unearthed thousands of reports of extraordinary happenings, including cases of spontaneous human combustion, inexplicable flash floods and falls of red rain. Fort offered a characteristic non-explanation for such phenomena saying, 'we are being played with'

happy childhood, Fort suffered much physical punishment at his father's hands, which made him hate authority. His rebellions prepared him for a life questioning authority and dogma. When he was 18 he left home to hitch-hike around the world in order, as he saw it, to put some 'capital into the bank of experience'. One day Fort boasted to a bedridden neighbour of his travels, but the man was not impressed. He too had travelled when he was younger, but it was only when he was confined to his room, he said, that he began to extract lasting values from his experiences. This impressed Fort very much and he later wrote: 'I [realised] that one should not scatter one's self upon all life, but center upon some one kind of life and know it thoroughly.' And that is what he did for the remaining 35 years of his life.

Fort's 'grand tour'

In 1897, at the age of 23, Fort read every scientific book and journal he could find and, within a few years, had amassed 25,000 notes on the infallible public face of authoritarian science. He burned them because 'they were not what I wanted.' He resumed what he called his 'grand tour', reading through the world's major newspapers and scientific journals and taking notes on small squares of paper in a cramped shorthand of his own invention. By 1915 he had several tens of thousands of notes, and he began writing two books. One was called X and explored the idea that life on Earth has been controlled by events or beings on Mars. The other was called Y. In this Fort presented evidence indicating that a sinister civilisation existed at the South Pole. In writing to his friend Theodore Dreiser, the influential American

novelist, he commented: 'You have at least one thing to be thankful for – I might have begun with A.'

Then Fort's luck turned – an uncle died leaving him just enough income to relieve him from the worry of earning his daily bread. Dissatisfied with the lack of publishing interest in his unusual books, Fort burned the manuscripts of X and Y and promptly began a third gleaned from his fabulous collection of notes. Dreiser was taken with the new work, *The book of the damned*, and persuaded his publisher to issue it.

When it appeared in 1919, most critics did not know what to make of it. It obviously presented a radical critique of contemporary science but it was fragmented, choppy and hard to follow. Eminently quotable, by turns compassionate, violent, poetic, ironic and deceptively wise, it was written in a difficult stream-of-consciousness style.

Fort was a cynic about scientific explanations. He observed how scientists argued for and against various theories, facts and kinds of phenomena according to their own beliefs rather than the rules of evidence. He was particularly appalled at the way in which any datum that did not fit one scientist's view, or the collective view, was ignored, suppressed, discredited or explained away. Fort called such rejected data 'the damned' because they were 'excommunicated' by science, which acted like a religion.

Fort did not like to be told what to think and expected his readers to think for themselves as well. His favourite technique was to state the bald facts flatly and then criticise them according to their validity and usefulness. Then he would present some 'expert's'

According to Fort almost anything can, and sometimes does, fall from the sky, to heap knee-deep around the bewildered onlooker. Among the many eyewitness accounts are descriptions of the classic 'fire from heaven' (below) and rains of various artefacts, such as the steel ingots that fell on the citizens of Basel, Switzerland, in the late 15th century (right)

I now have a theory that, of themselves, men never did evolve from lower animals: but that, in early and plastic times, a human being from somewhere else appeared upon this Earth, and that many kinds of animals took him for a model, and rudely and grotesquely imitated his appearance, so that today, though gorillas of the Congo, and of Chicago, are only caricatures, some of the rest of us are somewhat passable imitations of human beings.

Travels of a prophet

The year after the publication of *The book of the damned*, Fort fell into a depression. He again burned his notes – which numbered 40,000 – and set sail for London. He could hardly contain his joy at the masses of material in the British Museum. In the next eight years he undertook his 'grand tour' several more times, at each pass widening his horizons to new subjects and new correlations. During this period, his belief in the eventuality of space travel developed, and he was sometimes to be heard giving forth on the subject to an uncomprehending crowd at Speaker's Corner in Hyde Park.

At this time Fort wrote *New lands*, the least successful and most cranky of his books. It was largely a satirical attack upon the pomposity of astronomers, who, he said, were 'led by a cloud of rubbish by day and a pillar of bosh by night . . . .' In 1929, Fort and his wife returned to New York and he began to work on *Lo!* He completed his last book, *Wild talents*, which dealt with the occult or psychic abilities of humans, in 1932, during progressive blindness and weakness. A few weeks later, on 3 May 1932, he was admitted to hospital; he died within a few hours. He took notes almost to the end; the last one said simply: 'Difficulty shaving. Gaunt places in face.'

In 1931, the year before Fort's death, Dreiser and another novelist, Tiffany Thayer, organised a meeting to launch the Fortean Society. Fort was not altogether

case or explanation, and put in opposition to it a few, often fantastic, theories of his own based on precisely the same evidence. Whether the results gripped the readers' belief or sense of humour, he left up to them. For example, throughout his writings he expressed doubts about the Darwinian theory of evolution. Again, in *The book of the damned* he anticipated the von Däniken premise of 'ancient astronauts' by over 40 years. In thinking aloud about the strange vitrified forts of Scotland, he imagined that they had been destroyed in some ancient space war. 'I think we're property,' he wrote, and elaborated his meaning: 'That once upon a time, this Earth was No-Man's-Land, that other worlds explored and colonised here, and fought among themselves for possession, but now it's owned by something, all others warned off.' In *Wild talents* he elaborated:

A monstrous regiment

Long before the term 'psychic warfare' was coined, Charles Hoy Fort came up with the startling idea of harnessing psychic powers to conquer the enemy. He envisioned a fighting unit of 'poltergeist girls' on the battlefield.

This passage on such poltergeist activity from his last book (*Wild talents*, 1932) illustrates his typical style of throwing out his thoughts.

'. . . A squad of poltergeist girls – and they pick a fleet out of the sea, or out of the sky – if, as far back as the year 1923, something picked French airplanes out of the sky – arguing that some nations that renounced fleets as obsolete would go on building them just the same.

'Girls at the front – and they are discussing their usual not very profound subjects. Command to the poltergeist girls to concentrate – and under their chairs they stick their wads of chewing gum.

'A regiment bursts into flames, and the soldiers are torches. Horses snort smoke from the combustion of their entrails. Re-inforcements are smashed under cliffs that are teleported from the Rocky mountains. The snatch of Niagara falls – it pours upon the battlefield. The little poltergeist girls reach for their wads of chewing gum.'

Such a regiment would surely be the ultimate in deterrent weaponry.

surprised, but declined the presidency. He had actually put his objection to such an organisation several years before. In 1926 in a reply to the science fiction writer Edmund Hamilton's discussion of the growing number of people who had read Fort and wished to pursue his ideas, Fort wrote:

> That we shall ever organise does not seem likely to me . . . . The great trouble is that the majority of persons who are attracted are the ones we do not want; Spiritualists, Fundamentalists, persons who are revolting against science, not in the least because they are affronted by the myth-stuff of the sciences, but because scientists either oppose or do not encourage them.

Nevertheless, Thayer founded the Fortean Society and it enjoyed much success in its early years. But because Thayer championed ever more cranky ideas – a flat Earth, for example – the society, and its journal *Doubt*, petered out with his death in 1959.

Method in his madness?

Today we can appreciate the method in Fort's madness as we see some of his wildest data in a wider context. For example, we acknowledge him as one of the main influences upon the developing study of UFOs, not least because such writers as Eric Frank Russell and Vincent H. Gaddis were originally members of the Fortean Society. Gaddis was already contributing articles on mysterious crafts and lights in the skies before the famous sighting by Kenneth Arnold at Mount Ranier, Washington, USA, in 1947, when the term 'flying saucers' was coined. Thirty years previously Fort had begun to collect notes on lights and dark objects seen dancing, speeding and hovering in the skies over many countries. He wondered then if they were the aerial transports of alien visitors – 'super-constructions' as he called

Top: a sea monster, one of the many 'impossible' creatures listed by Fort as having been reported by sober, reliable witnesses – and dismissed totally by equally 'reliable' scientists

Above: Theodore Dreiser (1871–1945), the American writer who was passionately concerned with projecting Fort as an immensely readable and worthwhile researcher. As he wrote in his review of Fort's *Lo!* (right): 'Charles Fort is the most fascinating literary figure since Poe.' But unlike Poe's works, Fort's were non-fiction – or were they?

them. He also conjectured that some of them might be little-known forms of natural phenomena.

Fort must also be credited with the discovery that UFO sightings come in 'flaps', as exemplified by the series of sightings of mystery airships across America (1896–1897), and Britain (1904–1905 and 1908–1909). At those times, no known airship could match the mystery crafts' speeds, design or powerful lights. It was this groundwork that prepared the early ufologists for the study of the wave of 'missile-like meteors', later called 'ghost rockets', that were sighted throughout northern and western Europe in 1946. If there were aliens with technologies in advance of ours, Fort mused in *New lands*, they might be able to project images of themselves onto Earth. Or, they might have appeared on Earth in person in earlier times and been taken for apparitions or demons. So that if we consider the history of apparitional phenomena, could not, as Fort asked, many of the 'appearances [be] beings and objects that visited this Earth, not from a spiritual existence, but from outer space'? Although Fort was being deliberately provocative, this passage does anticipate the psychological, psychical and paraphysical dimensions of close encounter experiences of the 'contactees' of today.

Another fundamental contribution by Fort to contemporary theorising is his notion of teleportation as a primary force for distribution of matter, objects and life forms throughout the Universe. From his acquaintance with the literature of Spiritualism, he was aware of the phenomenon of

LO! by CHARLES FORT

Acclaimed by

THEODORE DREISER

"Charles Fort is the most fascinating literary figure since Poe. His books thrill and astound me."

BOOTH TARKINGTON

"He is colossal, magnificent . . . Anyone interested in unorthodoxies, who enjoys having his imagination staggered and his mind dazzled, should read this vigorous and astonishing book."

JOHN COWPER POWYS

"I am struck sharply and starkly by the curious genius of Charles Fort. He creates that curious awe in the mind, in the presence of this inexplicable universe, which Goethe in *Faust* declares to be one of man's noblest attributes."

It was the operation of this force of teleportation within the sphere of living creatures that most fascinated Fort. He could explain falling fishes or frogs in terms of the animals being whisked away from wherever they were abundant to some point in a distant sky, from which they then proceeded to fall. This could account for the sudden appearance of animals far from their usual habitats, or the appearance of fish in a freshly dug pond in spring, 1921. The teleportive force might even come under human control from time to time: poltergeist phenomena, levitation, bilocation or psychokinesis could occur consciously. Many of these ideas were eagerly seized upon by such American science fiction and fantasy writers as Robert Heinlein, Theodore Sturgeon, James Blish, Charles Harness, August Derleth and Philip Jose Farmer, some of whom were also members of the Fortean Society.

Over a two-year period when he was in his early fifties, Fort wrote a series of four letters to the *New York Times* in which he maintained that aliens were patrolling the skies. They were regarded as crank letters. When he died, the same dignified newspaper called him a 'foe of science' in its obituary on him. Fort would probably have expected such an epithet from people who had never tried to understand him. But his reputation has leaped over the *Times*'s opinion. Today some people regard Charles Hoy Fort as a prophet and visionary – and few who have studied him are prepared to dismiss him entirely.

'apports' – objects that materialise in the seance room. He felt that apports had an affinity to the appearances and disappearances of people, things and animals, the mysterious transportations and flight of objects usually, but not necessarily, during 'hauntings', and the phenomena of things and animals that fall in the open air in improbable circumstances. Fort coined the word 'teleportation' to describe such phenomena when he was writing *The book of the damned*. He saw teleportation as one of the basic forces of nature. It not only distributed life forms among the planets, but actually shifted materials of which they were built and shaped their environment. In the early days, wrote Fort, this force would have been extremely active. But as life and matter became more equally distributed among the inhabitable worlds, and became better established in their new homes, the need for the force would lessen. Eventually, he said, it would become vestigial, functioning erratically: 'The crash of falling islands – the humps of piling continents – and then the cosmic humour of it all – that the force that once heaped the peaks of the Rocky Mountains now slings pebbles at a couple of farmers near Trenton, New Jersey.'

A wise fool

Did Charles Fort stumble onto some cosmic understanding as a result of collecting anomalous phenomena ignored by scientists?

THE PUBLICATION OF *The book of the damned* by Charles Hoy Fort in 1919 changed the standard of reporting of anomalous phenomena in American newspapers for the better. Nonetheless, there was a sting in the tail. For whenever journalists reported a sighting of a sea serpent, or a home disrupted by a poltergeist, or a shower of frogs, they would comment to the effect that 'here is another datum for the archenemy of science, Charles Fort.'

This unfortunate reputation of Fort as an enemy of science lingers. Anyone who has read his books, however, must disagree. Fort was extremely well-versed and up to date in nearly all branches of science in his day and understood the scientific method, the rules of evidence and proper scholarship. Fort had looked closely at the great and impressive edifice of science and found it full of cracks. He found scientists who made pontifical pronouncements without bothering with the facts of the case, who substituted dogma for true scientific enquiry, who suppressed, ignored or explained away embarrassing data. He felt that anomalies held significance for science and should be studied. To understand that significance, it is necessary to look briefly at how science develops and changes.

Above: a UFO photograph of 1965, listed in the Condon Report as a possible fake. Fort's interest in and notes on UFOs helped set the stage for the development of present-day ufology

Right: Galileo demonstrates his telescope to Florentine nobles. The first person to use a telescope for the study of the skies, Galileo made a series of important findings in the early 17th century – but his work was rejected by hide-bound scholars and the then all-powerful Church because it went against accepted ideas

The history of science is not one of orderly progression; it resembles more a battle, full of seemingly chaotic advances, retreats and skirmishes. This view of disorder and accident in scientific progress has been endorsed in one of the essential works on the history of science, *The structure of scientific revolutions* (1962) by Thomas Kuhn. At any time in its history, says Kuhn, a science is the prisoner of the 'basic preconceptions' of the day. These preconceptions are limiting factors, which he calls 'paradigms'. But paradigms are essential to the formal expression of a science because they serve as models or structures with which to organise whole areas of knowledge and to provide the context for explanations.

Kuhn shows that the rise of a new paradigm in science, and the demise of the outdated one, is not the 'graceful surrender' by fair-minded individuals that science propagandists would have us believe. It is often as painful and protracted as any religious or political revolution, and for much the same reason. Scientists are human beings with all the weaknesses and worries of human beings. They have a great deal invested in their job, their status and their credibility – factors of more value to their security than the ideal of an open mind. Above all, they tend to be loyal to the familiar paradigm.

The classic example of reluctance to accept something new is that of the group of Italian scientists who refused to look through Galileo's telescope lest they, like the Jesuit Clavius, be tempted to abandon their comfortable view of a geocentric Universe on seeing Jupiter's satellites through the instrument. Indeed, the revolutions of moons about Jupiter, the model for the new idea of the solar system, remained in contention for

many years after Galileo proposed the idea.

A new paradigm, or the data that leads to it, can seem threatening, even sinister. So the body of orthodox science behaves like an invaded organism and closes ranks against the 'infectious' data. Eventually the anomalies mount up and there comes a time when they can no longer be ignored. There ensues a crisis period during which whole fields of science are broken apart and the pieces reassembled incorporating the new data. What was once anomalous is now accepted or explained as a self-evident fact. Recurrent crisis is not only typical of scientific progress,

Above: this illustration from Marco Polo's account of his Asian travels in the 13th century shows the fantastic creatures that, he had heard, lived in India. Such travellers' tales are still part of the data base of anomalous phenomena

Below: Antoine Lavoisier, the 'father of modern chemistry'. Despite his distinction as a scientist, he dismissed out of hand the existence of meteors – and helped prevent their being studied by science for decades

Kuhn says, it is essential to it. In *Lo!*, Fort called science 'the conventionalization of alleged knowledge', explaining: 'it acts to maintain itself against further enlightenment, but when giving in, there is not surrender but partnership, and something that had been bitterly fought then becomes another factor in its prestige.'

The main aim of orthodox science is to consolidate the field of knowledge, not to seek out oddities of fact or theory. Repeatability and regularity are preferred to anomalousness.

Age-old oddities

The study of strange phenomena is clearly not in the same stage of development as mainstream science. In the field of 'anomalistics', as some American scholars call it, collections of oddities have long abounded, however. Many of the works of the Greek philosophers such as Pliny, Pausanias and Athenaeus are rich in Forteana. So are the writings of travellers such as Ibn Batutah and Marco Polo and of the compilers of early bestiaries and natural histories such as Olaus Magnus and Edward Topsell. Their work forms a vast data base on the subjects currently lumped under the heading of 'the unexplained'.

If this data base corresponds roughly to what Kuhn calls the 'morass' of data at the early point of a science, then we are only awaiting the coming of that organising paradigm to begin our transformation into scientists. Once again Fort points the direction, giving us a particularly useful expression. He says that orthodox science is, by its own definition, 'exclusionist'. A scientific experiment, for example, is an attempt to isolate something from the rest of the Universe. The flaw of orthodoxy lies in its attempts to put things into units or categories. Yet anyone who has seriously investigated strange data knows that they defy categorisation. Exclusionist science functions well enough but bases its criteria on arbitrary decisions. As science progresses, such distinctions become obsolete and collapse. Thus in the early 19th century many biologists still regarded living things as essentially different from non-living things: for these 'vitalists' there was an unbridgeable gap between the animate and inanimate worlds. But from 1828 onwards, as chemists learned to synthesise organic

Left: Werner Heisenberg, a Nobel prize-winner for his work in nuclear physics. The quantum theory, to which he made a great contribution, was not taught at one of Britain's ancient universities for 30 years after its formulation – a striking example of how scientists will sometimes resist new ideas from even their most distinguished colleagues

Below: a prism creates a colour spectrum when light passes through it – a fact that led to the theory that light was made up of waves, although Newton, who first performed this experiment, believed that light was composed of particles. Today light is considered to behave as a wave form *or* as a stream of particles (photons), depending on the experimental circumstances. This progression in the way that scientists explain light shows how a paradigm can change

compounds (compounds such as urea or acetic acid, which are produced by living organisms), the distinction between the animate and the inanimate lost its fundamental importance for chemists, and to present-day scientists seems little short of superstition. They tend to forget that many of the dividing lines drawn by today's science – such as that between mind and matter, for example – may be redrawn or abandoned; and they slavishly accept or reject data by criteria that are, at best, transient. It is clear that this arbitrary structure predetermines how we interrogate the Universe – and how we interpret its answers. The German physicist Werner K. Heisenberg wrote: 'What we observe is not nature itself, but nature exposed to our method of questioning.' So light will behave like a wave or a particle according to the context in which it is investigated. Or, as the duck said with peculiar logic in *Alice in Wonderland*: 'When *I* find a thing, it's usually a frog or a worm.'

The barriers between the acceptable and unacceptable in science are changing all the time. What is magic or superstition to one era may become the science of the next. The great French chemist Antoine Lavoisier told the Academy of Sciences in 1769 that only peasants could believe stones could fall from the sky, because 'there *are* no stones in the sky.' His influence prevented scientific study of meteorites – the 'stones from the sky' – until 1803.

But some barriers are breaking down. Today's life sciences contain much rehabilitated folklore: old herbals have been used for new pharmaceuticals and the practices of shamans have been adapted for new treatments. Apparitional phenomena, once the preserve of theologians and demonologists, are now the subject of psychical research and psychology. A number of Fort's special correlations – strange lights on the Moon, curious aerial lights and sounds that accompany or precede earthquakes, lunar periodicities in biological processes and behaviour, lake monsters and UFOs – are all matters of serious academic study today.

In answer to how strange phenomena could relate to the main body of science, Fort suggested that it was science that would make the move to assimilate anomalous phenomena by adopting a more radical, inclusive approach. Inclusionists would 'substitute acceptance for belief', he said, but only temporarily until better data or theories arose. This is exactly what true scientists do, of course, because for them enquiring after the truth is more important than being right or first. Inclusionism would recognise a state of existence in which all things, creatures, ideas and phenomena were interrelated and so 'of an underlying oneness'. From his thousands of notes, Fort came to the realisation that the Universe functioned more like an organism than a machine and that, while

Left: Charles Hoy Fort at his super checkerboard. He invented a game called super checkers (draughts), which was so complicated that it usually took all night to play it to the end

Below: a medieval fool. The jester poked holes in the customs and beliefs of his society – a role Fort played in ridiculing the scientific establishment of his day

Fortean Times. The only scientific body concerned with anomalous phenomena is the Center for the Study of Short-Lived Phenomena, formerly part of the Smithsonian Institution in Washington DC, USA. It is now a successful self-funding venture. The establishment in London in 1981 of the Association for the Scientific Study of Anomalous Phenomena (ASSAP) may be a sign of hope for interdisciplinary studies of all sorts in the future.

One day, when orthodox science widens its circle of attention, the task of assimilating Fortean phenomena will have been made easier by the dedicated collectors of obscure and weird data. Their true function, in relation to mainstream science, is elegantly stated in a line from Enid Elsford's book on the medieval fool: 'The Fool does not lead a revolt against the Law; he lures us into a region of the spirit, where . . . the writ does not run.'

For the present author at least, Charles Hoy Fort was science's fool.

general principles applied universally, eccentricities, deviations and anomalies were the inevitable result of local expression of those principles. This almost mystical view anticipates C.G. Jung's notion of the collective unconscious and similar beliefs that appear in the cosmologies of primitive and animistic religions. Yet another theory in which the world is seen as functioning more like an organism than a machine emerged in 1981 – Dr Rupert Sheldrake's revolutionary principle of formative causation. This appears to offer philosophical tools for exploring continuity and synchronicity by postulating a resonance between forms of similar structure, whether living or not, that operates outside time and space.

Portents of change

In earlier times, most cultures had an appreciation of anomalies that we have lost. They also had some framework in which to study them, usually as omens or portents of social change, as C. G. Jung suggested UFOs might be. Priests in rural Scandinavia in the late medieval period were obliged to report to their bishops anything contrary to the 'natural order'. Their chronicles that survive are treasure troves of sea serpent sightings, falls of mice and fish, animal battles and other strange phenomena.

Today such stories are absent from the scientific journals, where Fort found them, and are used as small filler paragraphs in the newspapers, written inaccurately and for laughs. Apart from a few excellent specialist magazines, the only regular journals devoted to the reporting and discussion of Fortean phenomena are two American publications, the *Journal* of the International Fortean Organisation and *Pursuit*, published by the Society for the Investigation of the Unexplained (SITU), and Britain's independent

Right: the simply marked grave of Fort at Albany, New York, where he was born

In 1908 a vast area of Siberia was devastated by the explosion of a huge fireball. Trees were scorched and felled, and the skins of many animals broke out in scabs. Could this have been a nuclear explosion? IAN RIDPATH analyses the facts

The great Siberian

ON THE MORNING OF 30 JUNE 1908, farmer S. B. Semenov was sitting on his porch in the isolated Siberian trading station of Vanavara, 500 miles (750 kilometres) north-west of Lake Baykal. It was still only 7.15 a.m., but the day was already well under way; the Sun rises early in midsummer this far north. Nearby, Semenov's neighbour P. P. Kosalopov was pulling nails out of a window frame with pincers. Neither man could have had an inkling of the drama they were about to witness.

Suddenly, Semenov was startled to see, towards the north-west, a brilliant fireball that 'covered an enormous part of the sky'. Semenov twisted in pain, for the fireball's heat felt as though it were burning his shirt. Next door, Kosalopov dropped his pincers and clasped his hands to his ears, which felt as though they were burning. He first glanced at his roof, suspecting it to be on fire, then turned to Semenov. 'Did you see anything?' Kosalopov asked. 'How could one help but see it?' replied the frightened Semenov, still stinging from his burns.

A few seconds later, the blinding, bright blue, fireball, trailing a column of dust, exploded 40 miles (65 kilometres) from Vanavara with a force that knocked Semenov off his porch, where he lay unconscious for a few

seconds. On coming to, he felt ground tremors that shook the entire house, broke the barn door, and shattered windows. In the house of Kosalopov, earth fell from the ceiling and a door flew off the stove. Sounds like thunder rumbled in the air.

The great Siberian fireball of 1908 was an event so exceptional that it excited a controversy that continues to this day. Explanations for it range into the realm of the bizarre, including the remarkable hypothesis that it was caused by nothing less than the emergency landing of a nuclear spacecraft,

The aftermath of the explosion on 30 June 1908 of a huge fireball that 'covered an enormous part of the sky' over Tunguska, Siberia (map inset, right), must have looked much like a forest fire (top); for up to 20 miles (30 kilometres) around the site of the explosion, trees were blown down, and the intense heat of the blast set the forest alight

Thirteen years after the Tunguska explosion, Soviet mineralogist Leonid Kulik (above) led an expedition to the site, travelling by horse-drawn sled and boat (right). His route is shown in the map (above right). Kulik found dramatic evidence of the blast – whole forests of scorched and uprooted trees (left)

reball

perhaps even of extra-terrestrial origin.

The area on which the object fell, in the valley of the Stony Tunguska river, was sparsely inhabited by the Tungus, a nomadic, Mongol-like people who herded reindeer. Near the centre of the fall, north of Vanavara, several Tungus were thrown into the air by the explosion, and their tents were carried away in a violent wind. Around them, the forest began to blaze.

As the dazed Tungus cautiously inspected the site of the blast, they found scenes of terrifying devastation. Trees were felled like matchsticks for up to 20 miles (30 kilometres) around. The intense heat from the explosion had melted metal objects, destroyed storehouses, and burned reindeer to death. No

living animals were left in the area but, miraculously, no humans were killed by the blast. There were also reports that a mysterious 'black rain' had fallen in the area.

The effects of the Tunguska blast were seen and felt for 600 miles (1000 kilometres) around. Reports from the district of Kansk, 400 miles (600 kilometres) from the blast, described boatmen being thrown into the river and horses being knocked over by shock waves, while houses shook and crockery crashed off shelves. The driver of the Trans-Siberian express stopped his train for fear of a derailment when the carriages and rails began to shake.

Other effects were noted around the world, but their cause remained a puzzle for a long time, as news of the fireball and explosion did not become widely known for many years. Seismic waves like those from an earthquake were recorded throughout Europe, as well as disturbances of the Earth's magnetic field. Meteorologists later found from microbarograph records that atmospheric shock waves from the blast had circled the Earth twice.

Echoes of distant Siberia

A woman in Huntingdon, England, wrote to *The Times* to report that the night skies were so bright that shortly after midnight on 1 July 'it was possible to read large print indoors. . . . At about 1.30 a.m. the room was quite light, as if it had been day. It would be interesting if anyone would explain the cause of so unusual a sight.' But, at that time, no one *could* explain.

Similar eerie night-time effects were noted over much of Europe and western Asia after the fall. Reports from this area record nights up to 100 times brighter than normal and crimson hues in the sky, like the glare from fires towards the north. The strange lights did not flicker or form arches like the *aurora borealis*; they were like effects that followed the outburst of Krakatoa, which injected vast clouds of dust into the atmosphere.

At the time of the Tunguska fall, Russia was entering a period of major political upheaval and the national press did not give any coverage to what it saw as a minor event in a remote part of the empire. Despite the exceptional nature of the Tunguska event, news about it remained buried in local Siberian newspapers until 13 years later, when word of it reached a Soviet mineralogist, Leonid Kulik.

Kulik had a particular interest in fallen meteorites, not least because of the rich source of iron they could provide for industry. He became convinced that the object that had fallen on 30 June 1908 in the valley of the Stony Tunguska river was an iron meteorite even larger than that which formed the vast Barringer crater in Arizona 25,000 years or so ago.

After years of planning, Kulik set out in 1927 on an expedition to reach the site of the

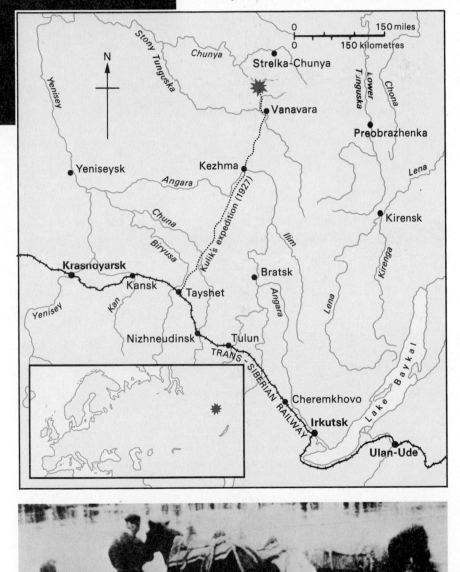

Tunguska fall. From the railway town of Taishet, Kulik and his team crossed 400 miles (600 kilometres) of frozen *taiga* by horse-drawn sled until they reached Vanavara. There, they heard the remarkable stories of the inhabitants, convincing Kulik more than ever that he was on the track of a truly enormous meteorite.

A sudden snowfall held up progress for over a week. On 8 April, Kulik, a colleague, and a local guide set out on horseback on the final leg of the journey. They marched northwards through scenes of increasing devastation: birch and pine trees lay on the ground where they had been uprooted by the force of the shock wave 19 years before. Many of the trees had been scorched or even set alight by the same intense heat that farmer Semenov had felt in Vanavara.

Surveying the blast area from a ridge, Kulik wrote:

From our observation point no sign of forest can be seen, for everything has been devastated and burned, and around the edge of this dead area the young twenty-year-old forest growth has moved forward furiously, seeking sunshine and life. One has an uncanny feeling when one sees 20- to 30-inch [50- to 75-centimetre] thick giant trees snapped across like twigs, and their tops hurled many metres away to the south.

Visit of the god of fire
Kulik wanted to press on the remaining few miles to the centre of the blast, but the Tungus guides were superstitious, for their legends said the area had been visited by the god of fire, and they would go no further. Kulik had to return to Vanavara to recruit new guides, and another month passed before he arrived again at the devastated area and finally reached the centre of the fall – to

Above: members of the Tungus tribe, who were the most directly affected by the Tunguska explosion. They reported that, after the blast, many of their reindeer broke out in scabs – a fact that has led some scientists, assuming that the scabs were evidence of radiation sickness, to suggest that a nuclear explosion had occurred

Right: The area of devastation in Tunguska, showing the centre of the explosion and the direction of the fallen trees, together with three different suggestions of the path taken by the fireball. The path indicated by the solid red arrow was proposed by scientists K. P. Florensky and V. G. Konenkin, and is now generally considered to be the correct one

discover the great riddle of Tunguska.

Of the giant crater he had expected there was not a sign. Instead, he found a frozen swamp and a curious stand of trees which, despite being at the centre of the explosion, had escaped the effects of the blast that had levelled everything around them. Whatever object caused the explosion, it had never reached the ground. Although he returned to the area with bigger expeditions in subsequent years, Kulik never found any fragments of meteoric iron.

So if the Tunguska blast was not caused by the impact of an iron meteorite, what *was* the cause? In 1930, the English meteorologist Francis J. W. Whipple, assistant director of the Meteorological Office, proposed that the event had been caused by the collision of the Earth with a small comet, a suggestion supported by the Soviet astronomer A. S. Astapovich.

The popular view of a comet is a giant glowing ball of dust and gas trailing streamers for millions of miles, as with the spectacular Halley's Comet in 1910. But such brilliant comets are the exception rather than the rule. A dozen or more comets may be tracked by astronomers each year, but few or none of them ever become visible to the naked eye. Most comets are smaller and fainter than those illustrated in astronomy books; some comets, particularly old ones, may show no tail at all.

According to the most popular theory, a comet resembles a dirty snowball of frozen gas and dust. Old comets run out of gas to become nothing more than loose 'bags' of low-density rocks. Such an object would indeed cause a blazing fireball as it burned up by friction after plunging at high speed into the Earth's atmosphere, eventually shattering explosively as the forces of deceleration overcame its own strength. The mid-air blast of such an object would explain why there was no crater or meteorite fragments at

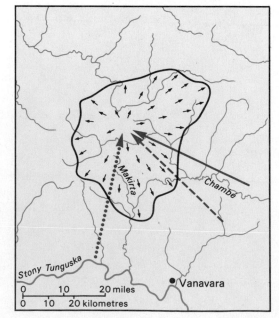

Right: the flight path of the Tunguska fireball in the area immediately surrounding the impact point, as reconstructed by Soviet ufologist Felix Zigel from the study of the damage created by the atmospheric shock wave, and the evidence given in a number of eyewitness accounts. The arrows through towns indicate the direction in which the object appeared to be travelling

Below: some of the evidence of large-scale destruction found by Kulik and his team 13 years after the blast: scorched trees, knocked flat by the force of the explosion or, where they were still standing, of stunted and scrubby growth

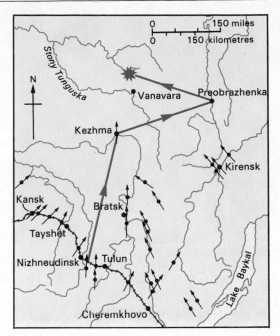

Tunguska. But critics of the comet theory argued that no comet had been seen in the sky before the Tunguska blast.

There has been a host of alternative explanations, including a bizarre suggestion that a mini black hole blasted into Siberia. According to astronomical theory, mini black holes, with the mass of an asteroid packed into the size of an atomic particle, could have been formed in the maelstrom following the Big Bang explosion that is believed to have marked the origin of the Universe. The passage of a mini black hole through the Earth would, according to University of Texas physicists A. A. Jackson and Michael Ryan, have all the observed effects of the Tunguska fireball – except that the mini black hole should have carried right on through the Earth and emerged in the north Atlantic, producing similar spectacular effects as it departed. Unfortunately for the theory, no such effects occurred.

Spacecraft from Mars?

Of all the theories for the Tunguska blast, the most controversial was put forward in 1946 by the Soviet science-fiction writer Alexander Kazantsev. Disguising his theory as a fictional story, Kazantsev proposed that the explosion over Siberia had been caused by the burn-up of a nuclear-powered spacecraft, perhaps from Mars. Kazantsev speculated that the aliens had come to collect water from Lake Baykal, the largest volume of fresh water on Earth. As the craft plummeted into the atmosphere it heated up by friction until the engines erupted in a mid-air blast like the Hiroshima bomb.

Soviet ufologists Felix Zigel and Alexei Zolotov have supported the exploding nuclear spacecraft idea. Zigel even proposed that the craft performed a crazy zig-zag as it desperately attempted to land, although none of the eyewitnesses actually reported seeing the fireball change course.

Another science-fiction writer, John Baxter, in his book *The fire came by*, published in 1976, followed Kazantsev in comparing the effects of the Tunguska explosion with those of the Hiroshima bomb – the strong thermal flash, the updraught of heated air that caused a 'fiery pillar', and the characteristic clump of trees that remained standing at the centre of the Tunguska devastation, as they had under the explosion point of the Hiroshima bomb.

There was even talk of deadly radiation at the site. One of the characters in Alexander Kazantsev's story speaks of a man who, shortly after examining the Tunguska blast area, died in terrible pain as if from an invisible fire. 'It could be nothing other than radioactivity,' explains the fictional character. In fact, there is no record that anyone died from the Tunguska blast – but the Tungus people reported that reindeer in the area broke out in scabs, which modern writers such as Baxter have attributed to radiation burns.

Expeditions to the area noted an accelerated growth of vegetation around the blast site, again attributed by some to genetic damage from radiation. There were reports in popular writings that radioactivity had been detected in the wood from the area, and an analysis of radiocarbon from tree rings in the United States by Nobel prize-winner Willard Libby showed an increase in radiocarbon following 1908. All of which seemed to indicate that the Tunguska explosion could have been nuclear.

This theory raises some alarming questions – for the Tunguska explosion occurred a good 30 years before the first nuclear tests. Who, or what, could have caused a blast of such proportions?

The Tunguska explosion was the disastrous end of a visitor from space. But was that visitor a spacecraft or a fragment of a comet?

SIBERIA, 30 JUNE 1908: a brilliant fireball blazed through the Earth's atmosphere, exploding at a height of 5 miles (8 kilometres) above the valley of the Stony Tunguska river with the force of a $12\frac{1}{2}$-megatonne nuclear bomb. According to one popular theory, the Tunguska explosion really was a nuclear blast, caused by the burn-up of a nuclear-powered alien spacecraft. But another leading theory says the Tunguska object was the head of a small comet. What evidence is there to back up these rival theories?

Important clues to the nature of the Tunguska explosion were obtained on three expeditions to the site, in 1958, 1961 and 1962, led by Soviet geochemist Kirill Florensky. His 1962 expedition used a helicopter to chart the disaster area. Instead of looking for large meteoritic fragments, as Leonid Kulik had done in the late 1920s, Florensky's team sifted the soil for microscopic particles that would have been scattered by the burn-up and disintegration of the Tunguska object. Their search proved fruitful. The scientists traced a narrow tongue of cosmic dust stretching for 150 miles (250 kilometres) north-west of the site, composed of magnetite (magnetic iron oxide) and glassy droplets of fused rock. The expedition found thousands of examples of metal and silicate particles fused together, indicating that the

Below: Willard F. Libby, one of a team who thought they had found an increase in atmospheric radioactive carbon-14 following the Tunguska explosion

Bottom: within a year of the explosion, Tunguska looked like this: fresh green growth pushing through the dead timber

Tunguska object had not been of uniform composition. A low-density stony composition containing flecks of iron is believed to be typical of interplanetary debris, particularly meteors ('shooting stars'), which are themselves composed of dust from comets. The particles spread north-west of the Tunguska blast were apparently the vaporised remains of a comet's head.

These actual samples of the Tunguska object should have been enough to settle the controversy once and for all. Florensky wrote about his expeditions in a 1963 article in the magazine *Sky & Telescope*. The article was entitled, 'Did a comet collide with the Earth in 1908?' Among astronomers, the comet theory has always been the front runner. In his article, Florensky said that this viewpoint 'was now confirmed'.

Radiation check

Florensky's expedition carefully checked for the existence of radiation at the site. He reported that the only radioactivity in the trees from the Tunguska area was fallout from atomic tests, which had been absorbed into the wood. Florensky's party also looked in detail at the acceleration of forest growth in the devastated area, which some had put down to genetic damage from radiation. Biologists concluded that only the normal acceleration of growth after a fire, a well-known phenomenon, had taken place.

But what of the 'scabs' reported to have broken out on reindeer after the blast? In the absence of any veterinary report one can only speculate, but most likely these were not

What really happened at Tunguska?

caused by atomic radiation but simply by the great flash of heat given out by the blast, which also set fire to the trees. Humans near enough to have felt the heat of the fireball showed no signs of radiation sickness, and remained alive and healthy when Leonid Kulik visited the site over a dozen years later.

Believers in the nuclear explosion theory quote investigations in 1965 by three American physicists, Clyde Cowan, C.R. Atluri, and Willard Libby, who reported a 1 per cent increase in radiocarbon in tree rings following the Tunguska blast. A nuclear explosion releases a burst of neutrons, which turn atmospheric nitrogen into radioactive carbon-14 that is taken up by plants along with ordinary carbon during their normal photosynthesis. If the Tunguska blast were nuclear, excess radiocarbon would be expected in the plants growing at the time.

To test this prediction, the American scientists examined tree rings from a 300-year-old Douglas fir from the Catalina Mountains near Tucson, Arizona, and also from an ancient oak tree near Los Angeles. They found that the level of radiocarbon in the rings of both trees had jumped by 1 per cent from 1908 to 1909. The picture is confused by erratic fluctuations of up to 2 per cent that exist in the levels of radiocarbon measured in the tree rings from year to year. Therefore a 1 per cent radiocarbon increase is not outside the range of normal fluctuations caused by natural effects. An important double-check was made by three Dutch scientists on a tree from Trondheim, Norway – much nearer the blast, where the radiocarbon effects would be expected to be more noticeable. Instead of a radiocarbon rise in 1909, they found a steady decrease around that time. Therefore the increase in American trees found by Cowan, Atluri and Libby must be due to local effects – and not to the Tunguska blast.

Pattern of destruction

Lastly, what about the clump of trees left standing at the centre of the Tunguska blast area, as were trees under the explosion point of the Hiroshima bomb, and the 'fiery pillar' seen after the explosion? In fact, these effects are not unique to a nuclear blast. Any explosion is followed by an updraught of heated air and a puff of smoke. Brilliant exploding fireballs happen frequently as chunks of solar system debris plunge into the atmosphere; fortunately for us, most of them are far smaller than the Tunguska object.

The clump of standing trees would be left behind by an aerial explosion of any kind, as shown by the scale-model experiments of Igor Zotkin and Mikhail Tsikulin of the Soviet Academy of Sciences' meteorite committee. They set off small explosions over a field of model trees, and found they were able to reproduce the pattern of felled trees including the central standing clump.

Therefore it seems that all the 'evidence'

The healing processes of the Siberian forest have not yet obliterated the scars of the 1908 explosion. Within a few years saplings had grown between the trunks strewn on the ground (top). But even today the fallen trees are still evident beneath a covering of moss and foliage (above)

adduced for a nuclear explosion at Tunguska is either misinterpretation or mischievous distortion.

Remarkably, the Tunguska event was repeated on a smaller scale over North America on the night of 31 March 1965. An area of nearly 390,000 square miles (1 million square kilometres) of the United States and Canada was lit up by the descent of a body that detonated over the towns of Revelstoke and Golden, 250 miles (400 kilometres) south-west of Edmonton, Alberta, Canada. Residents of those towns spoke of a 'thunderous roar' that rattled and broke windows. The energy released was equal to several kilotonnes of TNT.

Scientists predicted the meteorite's point of impact and set out to look for a crater, much as Leonid Kulik had done in Siberia half a century before. Like him, they were unsuccessful. Scanning the snow-covered ground from the air, the scientists were unable to find traces of the meteorite, or of a crater. Only when investigators went into the area on foot did they find that a strange black dust coated the snow for miles around. Samples of this dirt were scraped up, and proved to have the composition of a particularly fragile type of stony meteorite known to scientists as a carbonaceous chondrite. The 1965 object fragmented in mid-air, raining thousands of tonnes of crumbly black dust upon the snow. Significantly, witnesses to the Tunguska blast described just such a 'black rain'.

Clinching evidence for the cometary nature of the Tunguska object comes from the results of the latest Soviet expeditions to the site, reported in 1977. Microscopic rocky particles found in the 1908 peat layers have the same composition as cosmic particles collected from the upper atmosphere by rockets. Thousands of tonnes of this material are estimated to be scattered around the fall area. Along with these particles of rock from space were jagged particles of meteoric iron. The Soviet researchers concluded that the Tunguska object was a comet of carbonaceous chondrite composition. This comes as no surprise, for astronomers are finding that a carbonaceous chondrite composition is typical of interplanetary debris.

But if it was a comet, why was it not seen in

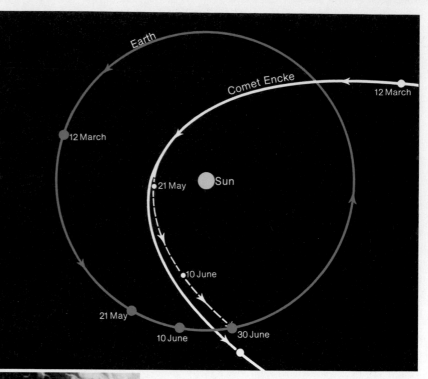

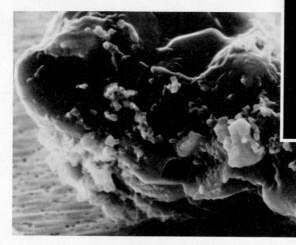

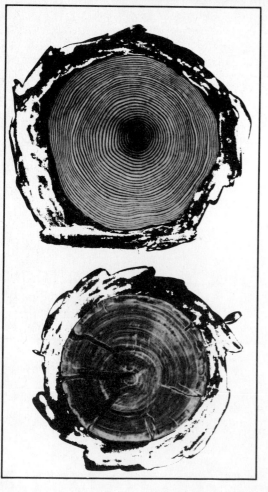

Top: how the Tunguska explosion may have happened. The comet Encke could have shed a rock fragment that was captured by the Earth

Above: this dust grain, magnified 10,000 times, was collected in the stratosphere. It is thought to have come from a comet

Left: the rings of recent Tunguska trees (top) are thicker than those of trees killed in the disaster (bottom). Some scientists claim that radioactivity from the explosion caused a spurt in plant growth

the sky prior to impact? Firstly, it always stayed close to the Sun so that it was lost in glare; and secondly, it was too small to have ever become bright enough to see even in a dark sky. Astronomers now believe that the Tunguska object was actually a fragment broken several thousand years ago from Comet Encke, an old and faint comet with the shortest known orbit of any comet around the Sun. A Czech astronomer, Lubor Kresak, pointed out in 1976 that the orbit of the Tunguska object, deduced from the direction and angle at which it struck the Earth, is remarkably similar to that of Encke's comet. Dr Kresak estimates that the body had a diameter of only about 100 yards (100 metres) when in space, and a mass of up to a million tonnes. Dust from its disintegration in the atmosphere caused the bright nights observed in the northern hemisphere in the period following the Tunguska event.

'The identification of the Tunguska object as an extinct cometary fragment appears to be the only plausible explanation of the event; and a common origin with Comet Encke appears very probable,' concludes Dr Kresak.

What is more, an event like Tunguska can happen again. Astronomers have found a number of small asteroids whose orbits cross the path of the Earth. For instance, in 1976 a direct repetition of the Tunguska event was avoided by hours as a previously unknown asteroid with a diameter of a few hundred yards swept past the Earth at a distance of 750,000 miles (1.2 million kilometres). Astronomers estimate that an object the size of the Tunguska comet hits the Earth once in about 2000 years on average. So it is only a matter of time before we are hit again – and next time it could do a lot of damage.

The strange world of twins

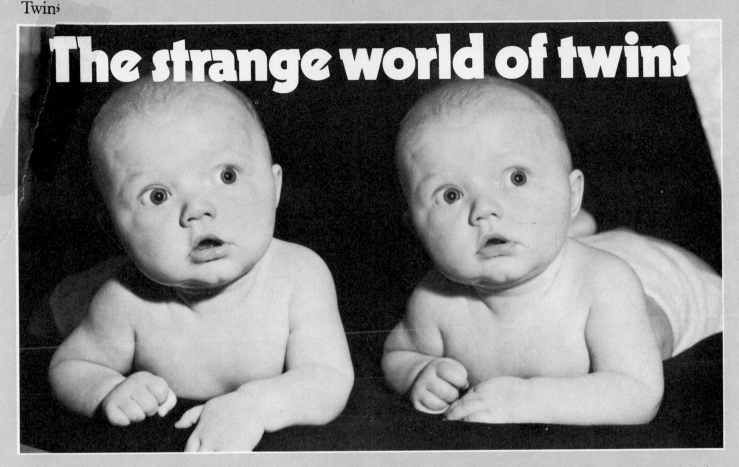

Identical twins who are brought up together are expected not only to look alike, but also to exhibit similarities of behaviour. Yet, as PAUL SIEVEKING shows, even twins who are separated at birth and reared apart still lead lives with astonishing parallels

OF THE HUNDRED MILLION or so twins in the world, about a third are *monozygotic*. This means that the babies have come from a single fertilised egg, which then divides into two in the womb. Such twins have identical sets of genes, and are alike in every detail – even down to their fingerprints – meaning that any differences between them must be exclusively non-genetic.

Those that have been brought up together naturally influence each other, so it is almost impossible to pinpoint to what extent their genetic blueprints shape their destinies. But there are on record about 80 pairs of twins who have, for one reason or another, been brought up separately, completely unaware of each other. A study of these twins offers fascinating clues to the relative significance of nature and nurture, heredity and environment. By studying such cases, we can gain some insight into how much of one's character is determined biologically, how much by upbringing and education – and discover how much is simply beyond our present understanding.

For example, identical twins Jacqueline

Identical twins come in all shapes and sizes, from the appealing American babies (above) to the unwieldy brothers attending the greatest ever 'get together' of twins at Barvaux, Belgium, in 1966 (below). The 24-year-old heavyweights pose with year-old identical twins, whose individual identities have not yet had time to develop. However, it seems likely that their parents will follow the tradition of dressing them similarly – at least until the twins reach adolescence, the time when more assertive twins tend to stress their individuality

and Sheila Lewis were adopted at birth by different families, and neither even knew the other existed. In June 1976, 26 years later, they were admitted to Southmead Hospital in Bristol, England, on the same day with the same rare hereditary skin disease. They were, by sheer chance, also put in the same treatment room. They soon discovered they were identical twins, even down to tiny details such as moles on their left knees, birthmarks on their necks and double-jointed little fingers. Both had suffered from pain in their left legs for several years and both had also had kidney trouble. Sheila's

and hated spelling; and as boys both owned dogs called Troy. Both had married women called Linda, divorced and then married 'Bettys'. Their first sons were named, respectively, James Alan and James Allan. Both families had taken their holidays for years at the same small beach in St Petersburg, Florida – driving there in Chevrolets. Both men had worked as attendants at filling stations, for the same hamburger chain, and part-time as deputy sheriffs. They had both taken up carpentry and technical drawing as hobbies. They were compulsive nail-biters; shared the same sleeping problems, smoking and drinking habits, and used the same slang words. Each is 6 feet (1.8 metres) tall and weighs 180 pounds (80 kilograms). After they met, their families noted similarities in speech patterns, mannerisms and posture.

At the age of 18, both the Jim twins started having tension headaches, which always began in the afternoon then turned into migraines. (They later used almost identical words to describe the pain.) Both stopped having them at the same age, then they started again for a time before stopping finally. It had never been thought that such a complicated migraine pattern could be 'programmed' by heredity. Moreover, both men have had confirmed or suspected heart attacks, had developed haemorrhoids, and both put on 10 pounds (4.5 kilograms) at the same time in their lives, and then lost it again.

In fact, synchronisation of ailments does seem to be a common feature between most twins, separated or not. Peter and Barry Ilott had their tonsils out together and both subsequently caught colds. 'It always follows the

husband had died on the same day that Jackie had divorced her husband.

1979 was a bumper year for the reunion of identical twins. It began with the 'Jim twins'. In August 1939 in Piqua, Ohio, USA, five-week-old identical twin boys were adopted by different families. One set of adoptive parents, Jess and Lucille Lewis, lived in Lima, while Ernest and Sarah Springer lived in Dayton 80 miles (130 kilometres) away. Both couples were told that the other twin had died; but Mrs Lewis learned the truth by accident six years later when she returned to probate court to complete adoption procedures. When she said that she had called the child James Edward, the court official said: 'You can't do that. They named the other little boy James.' The secret was out. But James he remained.

James Springer grew up believing his twin was dead, while James Lewis had no idea where his twin was, and hesitated for many years before tracing him painstakingly through the bureaucratic processes of the adoption courts. They were 39 when they finally met in February 1979. The level of synchronicity between them was quite astonishing. Both grew up with adopted brothers called Larry; at school both liked maths

Above: Jim Springer and Jim Lewis – the 'Jim twins' – with Lewis's adoptive mother. Separated at birth and reared by different families in Ohio, USA, they reunited at the age of 39 in 1979, and discovered an astonishing range of identical behaviour, such as calling their dogs Troy and having the same jobs in the same order. More incredible was the fact that both their adopted brothers had the same name. And both 'Jims' had married twice: the first time to a 'Linda' and the second to a 'Betty'. The odds against such coincidences happening through chance alone are overwhelming

same pattern,' said their mother. 'Barry is first to get the symptoms and within hours Peter has the same trouble.' Harold and Gerald Weitz also had their tonsils out together. In middle age, Harold had a heart attack, and Gerald followed suit a year later. Their doctor commented that their conditions were so similar that he could swear he was operating on the same person.

There have been several studies of separated twins, the largest being by the doyen of IQ testing, Sir Cyril Burt, who published the results of 45 years of research in 1966. He

Above: 300 pairs of identical twins take part in the *Frost Programme* on 17 January 1968 in London. At first glance each pair seems literally identical; they are – through habit or by request – wearing the same clothes and hairstyles, and seem to share the same physical mannerisms, such as the way they cross their legs or position their hands. However, a closer inspection reveals slight differences, enough, in most cases, to be able to tell the twins apart. But the big mystery about identical twins is not their appearance but the extraordinary degree of synchronicity in their lives

Left: Jeanette Hamilton and identical twin Irene Reid at their first meeting in 1981, 35 years after their adoption at birth. Uncannily they shared many experiences and even discovered they both had the same phobias – about water and heights

claimed to have studied 53 pairs of separated monozygotic twins. However, his reports were ambiguously phrased, giving no indication of the nature of the tests involved, and his IQ correlations were suspiciously uniform. His results were, it seems, 'cooked'. Burt's twin data was gathered between 1913 and 1939, and the bulk of his research papers was lost when a German bomb destroyed the basement records office of University College, London. His claim to have studied a further 32 cases between 1955 and 1964 is almost certainly untrue: much of his 1966 study appears to be a reconstruction of his pre-war work presented as post-war research. His assistants 'Miss Howard' and 'Miss Conway' simply never existed. In short, the father of British educational psychology was highly unscrupulous and his research on twins very suspect.

The other major studies of separated twins also suffer from grave defects, and lay the researchers involved open to the charge of 'hereditarian bias', that is, in their IQ studies they were prejudiced in favour of genetic rather than environmental influences. The 19 cases studied by Newman, Freeman and Holzinger in Chicago in 1937 were all apparently selected because they were very much like each other to begin with. Of the 37 allegedly 'separated' twins studied by Dr James Shields in London in 1962, many were actually looked after by different members of the same family, often living in the same town. The sample of N. Juel-Nielsen in Denmark in 1965 – 12 cases in all – was too small for scientifically valid conclusions to be drawn.

News of the Jim twins prompted psychologist Thomas Bouchard of the University of Minnesota, USA, to instigate a much more detailed study of separated twins than had previously been attempted. As a result of publicity, more than 30 cases of identical twins, separated in the first few months of their lives and not reunited until adulthood, have come to light, and each pair has been intensively studied for a week at Minnesota. (In mid 1981 the research was still being evaluated.)

A sample of this size offers a golden opportunity that may not arise again. This is because the likelihood of twins being separated at birth is diminishing as the stigma attached to illegitimacy disappears and fewer babies are 'put up' for adoption.

A surprising Sunday

One day in August 1979 Jeanette Hamilton opened the *Sunday Post* at her home in Paisley, Scotland, and saw her mirror image. The face staring up at her belonged to Irene Reid, who lived 300 miles (480 kilometres) away in Market Harborough, Leicestershire, and was looking for her long-lost twin. Jeanette and Irene spent the next three hours on the telephone making up for lost time.

Their unmarried mother had put them up for adoption in 1944. They discovered that they were both terrified of heights, had at one time led scout packs and worked part-time for the same cosmetics firm. They get a pain in the same spot on the right leg in wet weather. Both have such an aversion to water that when they go to the beach they tend to sit with their backs to the sea. They are compulsive calculators: if they see a lorry they will count the wheels on it. They suffer from claustrophobia, and hated having to enter one of the small testing rooms at Minnesota. Both have an extremely high rate of blinking, much higher than anyone else in the survey, but exactly the same as each other.

Also in 1979 Mrs Bridget Harrison of

Sir Cyril Burt (1883–1971), a distinguished British psychologist whose development of IQ testing led him to investigate the IQs of identical twins. His work implied there was, in almost every case, a perfect correlation. Unfortunately most of his records were destroyed in the blitz. Later, evidence came to light that undermined the validity of Burt's findings and seemed to prove that he had deliberately 'cooked' his results. Despite this, twins may indeed have very similar IQs

Leicester and Mrs Dorothy Lowe of Burnley, Lancashire, discovered they were twins. They had been apart since their birth in Lancashire in 1943. They had both married within a year of each other. One had called her son Richard Andrew, and the other called hers Andrew Richard. Bridget's daughter is Catherine Louise, Dorothy's is Karen Louise (and even then she was only called Karen to please a relative – Dorothy had really wanted to call her Katherine). Both had studied piano to the same grade, then stopped playing altogether after taking examinations at the same level. Both had had meningitis. Both collect soft toys, have cats called Tiger and wore almost identical wedding dresses. They leave their bedroom doors ajar; they wear the same perfume. They both kept a diary for just one year – 1960 – and the diaries they bought were the same make and design. The entries they made matched, day for day. Their mannerisms are identical, especially when they laugh. When they are nervous they cover their mouths with the same hand, and when talking they both put a hand on the back of their neck or pick at their nails. When Bouchard picked them up at Minneapolis airport in December 1979 he was astonished to see that both were wearing seven rings on one wrist, and, on the other, a bracelet and a watch. The Minneapolis study showed striking similarities between them in all areas, including their IQs, although, interestingly, the twin who had been raised in the more modest household did slightly better.

Bouchard and his team deny an hereditarian bias themselves, being more interested in environmental influences and individual differences, but admit that the scores on many tests were incredibly close.

On 27 July 1939 Helena Jacobsson, an unmarried Finnish student, gave birth to twin girls in Hammersmith Hospital, London. They were christened Dagmar (or Daphne) Margaret – who was the elder by just 12 minutes – and Gerda (Barbara). Both were adopted, Barbara growing up in London, and Daphne in Luton. They were 39 when they met in May 1979. It had taken Barbara five years' research to find her twin.

Barbara Herbert and her family live in southern England, while Daphne Goodship and her family live in the north. Both their adoptive mothers died when they were children. Both girls had fallen downstairs when they were 15, leaving them with weak ankles. Both met their future husbands at town hall dances when they were 16 and were married in their early twenties in big autumn weddings, complete with choir. Both miscarried their first babies, then each had two boys followed by a girl – though

Sharing the same fate

Daphne and Barbara with Professor Bouchard

Daphne had two more children later.

They like carving, though Barbara uses wood and Daphne soap. They have crooked little fingers and a habit of pushing up their noses, which they both call 'squidging'. They hate heights and are squeamish about blood. Both women giggle a lot. They enjoy novels by Alistair Maclean and Catherine Cookson, and both used to read the women's magazine *My Weekly* but stopped. Each has a minimal heart murmur and a slightly enlarged thyroid gland. Neither had ever voted – feeling too ill-informed about the political issues involved – except once when they were actually employed as polling clerks. At their reunion they were both wearing beige dresses, brown velvet jackets and identical white petticoats, and had tinted their greying hair almost the same shade of auburn. One difference was their weights: Daphne had been dieting and was 20 pounds (9 kilograms) lighter.

The only striking exception was of twins, one of whom was a fisherman in Florida, the other a CIA electronics expert. The fisherman was raised by an uneducated manual labourer, his twin by a highly educated man. Although both were great raconteurs, the difference in their IQs was considerable – about 20 points. It seems that the differences in background have to be very drastic before affecting the grown twins' IQs significantly.

Phobias were often shared – as we have seen in the case of Jeanette and Irene – which seems to disprove the conventional belief that these are the result of specific individual traumas. On the other hand, tests showed that most twins do not share the same allergies, so these seem unlikely to be genetic in origin. Smoking, too, seems to be an individual addiction. In several cases, one twin was a smoker and the other a non-smoker, but even so, the state of the lungs of the twins was very similar.

The astonishing similarity of names is one of the most unexplained of all the 'coincidences' involved, but the correspondence of children's names seems to be twice as mysterious because presumably the twin's husband or wife also had had a say in the matter. As for choosing wives with the same name (and in the case of the Jim twins not just once but twice) it would almost seem as if some kind of cosmic joker were responsible.

Then there is the odd phenomenon of *astro-twins* – people of the same sex born at the same time, *but not related* – who have led remarkably parallel lives. These cases offset some of the bizarre synchronicities of biological twins. For example: Goran Lundberg of Sweden was born on the same day as another Goran Lundberg. Both won scholarships to study in the USA in 1966. And both chose to attend Bethany College in Lingsborg, Kansas, where they met. Jacqueline Luscher and Elizabeth Boxxhard, born on the same day in the same town in

Above: identical twins Oscar Stohr and Jack Yufe, who were reunited in 1979. Theirs must be the most ironical of all separated-twin stories: Oscar had been reared as a fanatical Nazi – and Jack as a Jew

Below: English twins Bridget Harrison of Leicester and Dorothy Lowe from Burnley, Lancashire, who took part in Professor Bouchard's twin study. Aged 36 when they met for the first time, it almost seemed as if the same person had been living in two places at once, so strong were the similarities between them

Switzerland, married on the same day and also moved to Los Angeles simultaneously. Both had baby girls in the same hospital on the same day, attended by the same doctor.

But the most striking case of highly-synchronised, separated twins must be that of Oscar Stohr and Jack Yufe. They were born in Trinidad in 1933 and separated shortly afterwards when their parents quarrelled. Oscar was taken to Germany by his mother, where he became an ardent Nazi. With profound irony, Jack was reared in Trinidad by his father, a Jewish merchant. He attended the synagogue and became a King's Scout.

Identical: Nazi and Jew

In 1979, Jack read about the Jim twins and wrote to Bouchard suggesting that the scientists arrange a meeting between Oscar and himself to study them. When they met at the airport, they were both wearing wire-rimmed, rectangular spectacles and blue shirts with epaulettes, and both had short clipped moustaches.

The study revealed they had identical habits: they both flush the lavatory before and after using it; store rubber bands on their wrists; and prefer to dine alone in restaurants because they like to read over meals. Before eating, they clear the tables of all extraneous items. They both dip buttered toast into their coffee; read magazines from back to front; and like to scare people in lifts by sneezing very loudly. They have the same gait and way of sitting, and they speak with the same rhythms, even though Oscar speaks only German and Jack only English. So Nazi and Jew were brothers. However much scientists talk of 'hereditarian bias' and genetic versus environmental influences, one cannot help feeling that fate had a hand in this.

Double trouble

Some identical twins behave so similarly that, to a casual observer, they seem to share one identity, one personality.

INCREDIBLE THOUGH IT MAY SEEM, identical twins who are reared completely apart often exhibit more similarities of behaviour than those who grow up together. But when they reach their early teens most twins begin to develop a desire to be individuals, even if this is expressed only by dressing differently. Some, however, fail to do this, and grow up as if they were one person.

One of the most striking examples of this phenomenon became known in 1980 when the 38-year-old Chaplin twins, Greta and Freda, were brought before magistrates in York, England, charged with behaving in a manner likely to cause a breach of the peace.

Freda and Greta Chaplin of York, England, twins who exhibit 'mirror-imaging' to an uncanny degree. They seem to dress identically, but there are differences; for example, if Greta loses a shoelace from her left shoe than Freda will pull out her right shoelace. Similarly, when given two differently coloured bars of soap they suffered real distress until they cut the bars in half and shared them

They had, it was asserted, been harassing Mr Ken Iveson, once a neighbour of theirs, for 15 years: following him about, waiting for him outside the glassworks where he was employed as a lorry driver, shouting abuse at him and even hitting him with their handbags. This extraordinary fixation, however, was not the reason that psychiatrists, social workers and journalists were so fascinated by the case – for the twins spoke in what appeared to be *precise synchronisation*.

They exhibit other signs that seem to indicate that they are effectively one person. They are so alike in the way they think, speak, move and dress that children, believing them to be witches, have thrown stones at them in the street and adults have spat in their faces. They are a familiar sight in York – and are generally given a wide berth.

They wear identical grey coats, but as one originally came with green buttons and one with grey, they cut off two buttons each, and now both coats have two green and two grey. When given two different pairs of gloves they simply took one from each pair. Similarly a gift of two different coloured bars of soap caused them real anguish. They burst into tears, then solved the problem by cutting the bars in half and sharing them. When Greta got a prescription for bronchitis, Freda demanded the same medicine.

Speaking as one

The twins eat in unison, slowly raising forks and spoons together, finishing up one item of food before starting on the next. But most uncannily, they speak the same words at the same time, especially when excited or under stress; careful listening, however, reveals that the words of one come out a split second later than those of the other.

They also exhibit 'mirror-imaging', which is characteristically found in monozygotic or single-egg twins. In typical cases one twin is right-handed, the other left-handed; the whorls of the hair grow clockwise in one and anti-clockwise in the other; the left thumbprint of one almost matches the right thumbprint of the other, or similar wrinkles appear on opposite ears. Photographs of twins are most similar if one negative is flipped to produce a reversed image.

The Chaplins dress in mirror image of each other, although a casual observer would say they dress identically, and eccentrically, in their long skirts, clashing colours and headscarves. When Greta wears a bracelet on her left wrist, Freda wears one on her right, and if one breaks a shoelace, the other pulls a lace out of her opposite shoe.

Although the twins are difficult and unpredictable to interview, some journalists have managed to talk to them. Sue Heal from *Woman's Own* elicited this telling statement from them: 'We're so close that we're really one person. We know exactly what each other is thinking because we're just one brain.' Sue Heal remarked, 'You go gently for fear they'll disappear and leave you thinking you dreamed them up, like something from *Alice in Wonderland*.' She must have gained their confidence, however, because she did find out that they wear different underclothes.

And they do argue, sometimes hitting each other lightly with their identical handbags, then sitting sulking together for hours. If they believe they are the same person then how can an argument happen?

A closer examination of their history shows that their extraordinary togetherness was actively fostered by their parents, especially by their mother, who dressed them identically and allowed them no friends. They were not mentally abnormal and attended a secondary school near their York home. Teachers and fellow pupils remember them as neat, clean and quiet – and although

The Chaplins first achieved national notoriety in 1980 when they were brought before the York magistrates charged with persistently hounding Mr Ken Iveson (right) for 15 years. Their fixation with him became intolerable: they would lie in wait for him and shout abuse or hit him – this, it seemed, was their way of showing affection. It was their appearance in court that revealed the extent of their simultaneous behaviour (below), making them the focus for many newspaper and magazine articles, and the centre of a medical controversy

among the slowest students they could read and write as well as the others in their class. The deputy headmaster of the school has no doubts about what turned them into the disturbed adults they are today: 'It was clear that they had a doting mother who never allowed them any separate identity. . . . The other kids just saw them as a bit quaint. I don't think they were acutely isolated then or maladjusted.' They had not, at that point, begun to speak simultaneously.

Clearly their mother's attitude towards them had triggered off a pattern of abnormal behaviour, perhaps aided by their biological affinity. Both parents seem to have been uncommunicative and friendless and Mrs Chaplin is said to be obsessively houseproud. This emphasis on cleanliness may explain why the twins' only apparent pleasure is bathing together, grooming each other, washing each other's long hair. They are said to use an average of 14 bars of soap and three large bottles of shampoo each week.

The unfortunate Ken Iveson had grown up next door to the Chaplins; he married when the twins were two years old, but

continued to live at his parents' home with his wife and children. Neither he nor his parents had ever set foot inside their neighbours' house; they were never asked in and never saw anyone else pay social calls. Iveson would pass the time of day with the girls, who, isolated from the outside world, obviously took this as some kind of romantic encouragement. They rapidly became a nuisance and eventually, after 15 years, Iveson could take no more of it. Their case came to court.

The twins' parents had, it transpired, forced them to leave home. When asked about this, Freda and Greta reply as one: 'Something must have happened. Yes yes yes. Something strange. Must have happened.'

Mr and Mrs Chaplin refuse to talk to the press, and exactly why the twins left is not known. They now live in a hostel for the mentally handicapped.

Curiously, the local psychiatrists, called in by the court as expert witnesses, were baffled by the twins' case, describing it vaguely as 'a personality disorder'. Yet their behaviour towards Mr Iveson matches the textbook symptoms of *erotomania*, a form of schizophrenia that has been recognised as a clinical condition since the mid 1960s. Dr Morgan Enoch, of the Maudsley mental hospital in south London, has discovered that if one identical twin is schizophrenic then the other is also likely to suffer from the disease.

But does erotomania – or any form of schizophrenia – entirely explain the Chaplins' behaviour, especially their strange way of speaking? In their case there seem to be many highly influential factors – genetic, environmental, social – that have made them the objects of sympathy and derision that they are today.

Perhaps the Chaplins' peculiarity of speech is just one aspect of the way twins communicate with one another. Better

'Snap aduk, Cabenga, chase die-dipana' – at this mysterious command from one of the Kennedy twins, they both began to play with the doll's house. Grace and Virginia were believed to be mentally retarded until it was discovered that they had developed a language of their own, complete with extensive vocabulary and syntax. 'Poto' and 'Cabenga', as they called themselves, were investigated by speech therapist Anne Koenecke at the Children's Hospital in San Diego, California; she finally coaxed them into speaking a little English. Their curious, private language was an example of ideoglossia, which is developed most often by identical twins apparently to exclude the outside world

known is *ideoglossia*, the phenomenon in which two individuals, most often twin children, develop between them a unique and private language complete with highly original vocabulary and syntax.

It is, however, commonly confused with a sub-category, *twin speech* – a private collection of distorted words and idioms used, it is estimated, by 40 per cent of all twins because they feel isolated, or secretive, or both. Most twins tend to give it up at the age of three, although twin Robert A. Nelson wrote to the *New York Times* in 1932 that 'It is a matter of record in my family that when my brother and I first started to talk, and until we were well past six, we conversed with each other in a strange tongue of our own.' The only other person who could understand their particular speech was their brother, who was eight years older.

Identical twins Grace and Virginia were born in 1970 in Columbus, Georgia, USA, to Tom Kennedy and his German-born wife Christine. The day after the girls were born, Grace suddenly raised her head and stared at her father. Virginia did the same thing the next day. These strangely precocious acts, labelled 'convulsive seizures' by doctors, continued periodically for six months, in spite of treatment. At 17 months they apparently developed ideoglossia, beginning to speak rapidly in a language of their own – their only concession to English being 'mommy' and 'daddy'. They called each other Poto and Cabenga.

When the twins were two years old, the family moved to California, but there were very few other children in the neighbourhood for Grace and Virginia to play with. They were left to themselves or entrusted to their maternal grandmother, Paula Kunert, a

Not all children who share an intensely private world are twins. This tiny book (above) – so small that it can be read only with the aid of a magnifying glass – was one of the 'books' written by the children of the Brontë family. They created imaginary lands, Angria, Gondal and Glasstown, peopled with vivid characters and spoken of only in secret. Two of the children were particularly close: Charlotte (who later wrote *Jane Eyre*) and her brother Patrick Branwell. At least once they shared a strong telepathic experience when they were many miles apart

stern disciplinarian who still spoke only her native German.

In 1977 the speech therapists at the Children's Hospital in San Diego, California, began to study the twins, taping their conversation in the hope of learning something about the mysteries of developing language. Is it, they wondered, predominantly a product of genetic programming or a learned response to the world around them? A typical conversation between the girls would run:

'Genebene manita.'
'Nomemee.'
'Eebedeebeda. Dis din qui naba.'
'Neveda. Ca Baedabada.'

When the study began, the twins spoke no English, but gradually the therapists coaxed some out of them – which they spoke with a curious high-speed delivery. Anne Koenecke even tried to talk to them in their own language, but they just looked at her as if she were crazy.

'Snap aduk, Cabenga, chase die-dipana,' said 'Poto' masterfully. Having apparently issued a command she and 'Cabenga' instantly began to play with a doll's house.

Analysis of the tapes showed that their communication was something less than true ideoglossia. Many of the apparently new words turned out to be mispronounced words and phrases from German and English jammed together and said at high speed. However, a few words, such as 'nunukid' and 'pulana', remain unidentified. As the twins grew older they suddenly began to speak English – but they remain silent about the meaning of their once private language.

There are such strong links between some twins that they suffer simultaneous injuries – although miles apart – even dying at the same moment.

SINCE 1953, Professor Luigi Gedda of the Gregor Mendel Institute in Rome has studied more than 15,000 pairs of twins, and has elaborated a 'clock of life' hypothesis to account for the extraordinary correspondences in the lives of twins, which he describes in his book *Chronogenetics* (1978). There seems to be a whole range of major and minor manifestations of the mental bonds that link twins, from fairly commonplace telepathy – such as a simultaneous impulse to contact each other – to the actual transmission of pain and even physical wounds. Beyond these mental bonds are the even more astonishing cases of 'carbon-copy' accidents, which stubbornly defy rational or scientific explanation.

The 45 sets of twins of Haverhill, Suffolk – all were under the age of 20 in January 1980. This strange clustering of double births was particularly noticeable in a population of just 17,500, and naturally led to much speculation about the cause. One mother of twins said, 'I'm convinced it's the water. All my neighbours and friends have had twins.' Here the parents of the newest additions to the group tempt fate by toasting the camera – in water

In *The Corsican brothers* by Alexandre Dumas, Louis de Franchi is fatally wounded in a duel. At the moment he is shot his identical twin Lucien, 500 miles (800 kilometres) away, is struck with agonising pain. He feels as if a bullet has penetrated above his sixth rib and emerged just above his hip – exactly where Louis has been shot. This was fiction; but such strange bonds between twins have been reported many times in real life.

At 4.35 on a Saturday afternoon in July 1948 Alice Lambe, a 20-year-old typist, sat reading in the parlour of her family home outside Springfield, Illinois, USA. Suddenly, she felt an enormous jolt on the left side of her body, followed by a sharp stabbing pain and a feeling of shock. The impact of the unseen blow was enough to knock her off her chair. Before passing out, she cried out to her father 'Something's happened to Dianne!'

Dianne was her identical twin who had spent the day in St Louis, 70 miles (110

One in life and death

Professor Luigi Gedda with a colleague and twins at Gregor Mendel Institute in Rome. Gedda's researches into the curious correspondences in the lives of twins led him to postulate the existence of a 'clock of life' that, as it were, ticks in perfect synchronisation for both twins

kilometres) away. At 4.35 p.m. the train on which she was returning was derailed and Dianne was thrown across the carriage, landing on her left side. The next thing she knew was waking up in hospital. She had suffered two fractured ribs and severe concussion. She was off work for three weeks – but then so was Alice, whose continual complaints of stabbing pain eventually led to her being x-rayed. It turned out that she had fractured the same two ribs in the same place as her sister.

On 21 July 1975 Nettie Porter was involved in a car crash in Roseville, California. At the same time her twin sister Nita Hust, at work in a hospital 400 miles (640 kilometres) away, felt severe pains down her left leg, rolled up her trousers and was amazed to see bruises working their way up the left side of her body. The matron at the hospital bore witness to the spontaneous development of her marks, which corresponded to Nettie's injuries.

Ted Wolner and Harvey Stein give the following case in *Parallels: a look at twins* (1978). A young woman had an identical twin with acute appendicitis. She said: 'When they came to tell me this, they found me on the floor in pain. When the doctors took her into surgery, I could tell the moment when they started cutting and when they sewed her up. I was in the waiting room with my mother who said, "The operation should be over by now," and I said, "No, mother, the doctor has just started." And, indeed, the doctor later verified that the operation had been delayed.'

Sometimes the transference of injury can be fatal. Mrs Joyce Crominski wrote to the Australian magazine *Truth* about her identical twin sisters Helen and Peg. At 11.15 one evening Helen awoke, white-faced and screaming, with a terrible pain in her chest. Her parents sent for an ambulance but she died on the way to hospital – as did Peg, who had been in a car accident at exactly the same time as Helen awoke. The steering wheel had penetrated her chest.

Silvia Landa, aged five, burnt herself on a hot iron, and her twin Marta felt the pain 12 miles (20 kilometres) away. Both developed a burn scar on their right hands. Jayne Wilkinson, also five, fell and broke her nose – and her twin sister Claire had a nosebleed. Helen Fry, 13, was out shopping with her grandmother when she began to stagger about quite dazed and had to be taken home, where she fell asleep on the settee. Her twin Lorraine was in hospital for a minor operation, and both twins had experienced the anaesthetic. Alan Richmond shattered his knee in several places and his identical twin Arthur suffered the pain in his knee. As Ann Matthews's pregnancy progressed, her twin Ruth Harvey put on weight and suffered early morning sickness; she also shared the labour pains.

Dizygotic – or non-identical – twins also experience pain transference, even though genetically they are no more alike than ordinary brothers and sisters. On two occasions when Yvonne Green had a baby, her twin brother Christopher Gool had labour pains 300 miles (480 kilometres) away. Another time when Christopher, who is a policeman, hurt his arm in a brawl, Yvonne fell over and had to go to hospital to have her arm injuries treated.

Martha Burke of California, USA, suffered

Twins in twins

The phenomenon of the 'vanishing twin' has been studied by Dr Lucien Schneider of the University of Paris. This refers to cases where only one twin develops in the womb, while the other is reabsorbed by the mother's body. Sometimes, however, this fails to happen and one twin is born inside the other, as Isla Sneddon (left) discovered in 1980.

This 18-year-old student nurse from Glasgow, Scotland, complained of a cyst on her chest and was duly x-rayed. It was discovered that the 'cyst' was in fact her embryo twin, which had grown as big as a tennis ball and was preventing the blood supply reaching her right lung. If it had not been removed it would almost certainly have killed her. Isla said, 'I have always wanted a twin. It was a strange feeling. Perhaps I subconsciously knew.' Vanishing twins are, however, rare. From 1900 to 1979 there were only 11 similar cases reported throughout Britain.

from burning pains in her chest and stomach as her non-identical twin was burned to death in the Canary Island aeroplane crash of 1977, which claimed 582 lives. She sued the airlines for damages; not surprisingly her claim was unsuccessful. Mrs Sheargold went to hospital with a leg injury and her twin brother was kept awake by the pain. Later he cracked a rib, and *she* felt *his* pains.

Twins frequently give birth together. Jacky and Geraldine (née Herz) had babies within days of each other on 12 occasions. Many other twins have managed this feat at least once, often with greater synchronisation. In June 1970 Vera and Anita, twin daughters of Otto Heise of Einbeck, West Germany, who were quite unlike each other in looks, character and ways of life, were both taken to the same clinic and delivered of babies at the same moment. Jennifer Vickers and Patricia Harlow gave birth 'within hours' in 1974, and the following year Maureen Smith and Yvonne Gale gave birth within 23 minutes at Kingston Hospital, Surrey, England.

Death, too, can strike at the same time. Twins John and Arthur Mowforth, aged 66, were seized with chest pains on the same evening, 22 May 1975; they were rushed to hospitals in Bristol and Windsor respectively, and died of heart attacks in the evening. Twins Ida Torrey and Freda Palmer were born in Geronimo, Texas, in 1905. They died the same day in 1979, 350 miles (560 kilometres) apart. The same year, Frederick and Mary Ward of Portland, Maine, had fatal heart attacks at the age of 71, only 12 minutes apart. And in 1981, Margaret Cox and Florence Parrish of Georgia, born exactly two hours apart in 1894, died exactly two hours apart. Margaret, who had been born first, also died first.

Dr David Lykken and his colleague Dr Thomas J. Bouchard of the University of Minnesota, USA. Their extensive investigation of identical twins suggests that many possess a strong telepathic link

Three-month-old Lisa and Mark died within minutes of each other in Dublin in 1978. In April 1980, William and Wendy, who were two months old, died in Milwaukee, USA, and five days later another set of twins, Gaynor and Miracle (3 months) died in another part of the town. It seems that they were victims of the mysterious 'sudden infant death syndrome' (or, as it is more commonly known, 'cot death').

But even apparently trivial coincidences can be striking. One of the most frequently reported is of twins going off separately to buy dresses for a party and turning up in exactly the same outfits. This happened to Nettie and Nita in California: 'Both of us showed up wearing a yellow silk-screen print dress with a flared skirt, exactly identical; even our . . . shoes were the same.'

Identical twins Maureen Smith and Yvonne Gale gave birth to sons within 23 minutes of each other in Kingston Hospital, Surrey, on 15 January 1975. Does Professor Gedda's 'clock of life' account for such startling correspondences in the lives of twins?

Another, perhaps even more frequent event, is twins thinking of each other at the same time. Dr David Lykken of the University of Minnesota notes that when Nettie or Nita concentrates on her twin, the other soon telephones. This telepathic link is widely known but difficult to test by controlled experiment. Results are never quite conclusive. Thus we see from an undated clipping from the *Journal* of the American Association for the Advancement of Science that Doctors Duane and Behrendt wired up a pair of identical twins in separate rooms to record their brain waves, and found that a stimulus administered to the brain of one twin was simultaneously received by the other. Yet of 16 other pairs of twins later tested by the doctors only one pair responded similarly.

Twin telepathy is sometimes strikingly demonstrated by examination results. Twins Nancy and Ruth Schneider were born in Virginia, USA, in 1927. Sitting for college entrance exams in opposite corners of the room, they chose the same essay subject and wrote 'word for word' the same story, according to one of the invigilators, Dr Sara Roody.

In 1979, twins Elaine and Linda Beveridge graduated in social policy and administration at Leeds University. They sat for eight papers, getting identical marks on five. On one paper there was a difference of one mark, and on two papers and their dissertations, there was a difference of two marks. It had been the same with their 'o' and 'A' level examination results: exactly the same or different by only a few marks. Duncan and Alistair Dissett of Somerset got identical marks in all the eight 'o' level papers they took in 1980.

In January 1974 twins Frank and Jack Clatworthy, also from Somerset, were in adjoining hospital beds after being injured

Norris and Ross McWhirter, creators of *The Guinness book of records*. Both sub-lieutenants in the Royal Navy during the Second World War, they were detailed to separate minesweepers – which then collided with each other at Malta

within an hour of each other in separate accidents 3 miles (5 kilometres) apart on the same road outside Taunton, returning from the same party. Frank's car overturned, and Jack's went into a hedge (according to *The Times*), or overturned as well (according to the *Daily Mail*).

On 27 December 1972 the Jay twins, Helen and Catherine, had their handbags stolen in different BBC offices in London within five minutes of each other. They telephoned their bank simultaneously to cancel their stolen credit cards.

In 1973 Wendy Styles, 13, fell in the school gym and broke her left leg. She was waiting outside for the doctor when, a couple of minutes later, her twin sister Denise was also carried out, having broken her right leg.

The McWhirter twins, who created the *Guinness book of records*, were both sub-lieutenants in the Royal Navy in the Second World War. Norris was detailed to a minesweeper in Singapore, Ross to one in the Mediterranean. The vessels made their separate ways to Valletta, Malta, where they

collided. Similarly, twins George and Stephen Youngblood went off on motorbikes in October 1980, in opposite directions, to joyride along the backroads of Missouri, USA. Stephen died and George was injured when they met in a head-on collision.

Most of these incidents could be dismissed as the results of blind chance. Coincidences in general have the curious quality of seeming to be tremendously important, yet the nature of their significance remains frustratingly elusive.

Consider, finally, the story of Peet and Daan Snyman, identical twins from Pretoria in South Africa.

The Snymans, born in 1945, had appendicitis within a few days of each other and then meningitis at almost the same time. At the age of seven both were badly bitten in the leg by different dogs. They grew up to take such incidents for granted. In December 1964 Peet lost two fingers on his left hand while attempting to adjust the fan belt in his car. Two weeks later his twin lost the same fingers on his right hand in a car accident. This was particularly disastrous because by this time they were both professional guitarists. During the next 14 years both married and their lives diverged. Peet's wife had two children while Daan's remained childless.

But the pattern began again in February 1978 when Peet lost his right eye in a car accident. Eight months later Daan lost his left eye in another accident. Then, while Peet was out fishing, his line snapped and the lead sinker hit him in his good eye, making him totally blind. In 1980 his wife started divorce proceedings, saying she could not live with a blind man. In the circumstances, Daan began looking after his right eye very carefully, and wondered if his marriage would last much longer . . .

Right: Denise and Wendy Styles of Brading, Isle of Wight. In December 1973 the 13-year-old twins both fell and broke a leg in the school gymnasium within minutes of each other. Denise broke her right leg and Wendy her left: is this an example of 'mirror-imaging'?

Nothing but trouble

Curses have always been feared – with justice it seems, for disease, loss of loved ones and death have often befallen the victims. But is this coincidence or, asks PAUL SIEVEKING, could it be the direct result of knowing that one is cursed?

A CURSE IS AN INVOCATION of destruction or evil, part of the accustomed armoury of the priest, magician, shaman or ill-wisher. But do curses work and, if so, how? Swearing at someone gives vent to pent-up feelings; most psychologists would say that ritual curses do nothing more, *unless the victim is expecting trouble*. Sandford Cohen, a psychologist at Boston University, USA, is convinced from field research that curses can be lethal, because of the feeling of utter helplessness they can inspire. He sees a striking similarity between western Man dying from a fear of some disease generally believed to be fatal, and primitive Man dying from a witch doctor's curse.

Another explanation involves the 'tape recording' theory – that a thought can imprint itself on an object or person, and can be transferred to others. If the thought is malevolent, so is the effect. There do seem to be numerous cases of curse victims being totally sceptical of supernatural 'mumbo-jumbo', which nevertheless does nothing to save them from the effects.

Take the case of Robert Heinl junior, a retired colonel in the US Marine Corps. From 1958 to 1963 he served on Haiti as chief of the US naval mission, while his wife studied the voodoo religion. Afterwards, back in the United States, they wrote *Written in blood*, a history of Haiti that was openly critical of the ruling dynasty of François 'Papa Doc' Duvalier. Then they learned from a newspaper published by Haitian exiles that a curse had been placed on the book, probably after Papa Doc's death in 1971 by his widow, Simone.

At first, the Heinls were flattered that their book was thought to be worth cursing, but amusement soon turned to fear. First, the manuscript was lost on the way to the publishers, then it turned up four months later in a room the publishers never used. Meanwhile, the Heinls prepared another copy of the manuscript and sent it off for binding and stitching. The machine immediately broke down. A *Washington Post* reporter who was preparing to interview the authors was struck down with acute appendicitis. The colonel fell through a stage when he was delivering a speech, injuring his leg. And while walking near his home he was suddenly – and severely – bitten by a dog.

A Mycenaean funeral mask representing Agamemnon – one of the many sufferers from the ancient curse on the House of Atreus by Hermes. Agamemnon, the grandson of Atreus, was killed by his wife and her lover as a direct result

The omens continued, two involving the number 22, which Papa Doc considered a magic number. Finally, on 5 May 1979, the Heinls were on holiday on St Barthelemy Island, near Haiti, when the colonel dropped dead from a heart attack. His widow mused: 'There is a belief that the closer you get to Haiti, the more powerful the magic becomes.'

In Royal David's city

Curses, precisely laid down in many rituals, are still cast by priests in the major religions. In September 1981 Rabbi Moshe Hirsch, leader of the Neturei Karta, an orthodox Jewish sect, was threatening to invoke the 'Rod of Light' against the Israeli archaeologist Yigal Shilo if he persisted in excavating the biblical city of David, which the rabbi maintained involved desecrating a medieval Jewish cemetery. The archaeologists denied the existence of such a cemetery.

The Rod of Light ceremony involves the reading of a text based on *qabalistic* writings. The participants burn black candles, sound a ram's horn and invoke the name of the cursed man's mother. 'This ceremony is an absolute last resort,' said the rabbi. 'It has only been invoked twice in the last 30 years, both times with horrible consequences. There are many ways of dying, some less pleasant than others.' But unfortunately the

Left: Robert and Nancy Heinl, who fell foul of the Haitian dictator François 'Papa Doc' Duvalier and his wife Simone (below) while researching their book *Written in blood* – which was openly critical of Duvalier's regime – in the 1960s. The Heinls discovered that Simone Duvalier had cursed them and an extraordinary chain of events, culminating in the sudden death of Robert Heinl, followed. Coincidence? Nancy Heinl was in no doubt that the curse was responsible for their bad luck

by angry monks (see box).

There is a widespread ancient belief that no good will come from disturbing old stones or buried treasure – folklore worldwide is full of such tales. We can see the theme continuing in the enduring popularity of the idea of a mummy's curse in newspapers and films. Some researchers believe that such deep-seated and widespread beliefs, as part of the collective unconscious, can exert a material influence, thus bringing myths to life – and perpetually reinforcing them.

A heart of stone

The old castle of Syrie in Aberdeenshire, Scotland, has a legendary curse on it. A group of stones in the river there is known as the Weeping Stones, one of which is missing. It is said that no heir to Syrie will ever succeed until the missing stone is found.

In 1944 a 2-tonne 'Witch's Stone' was shifted from a crossroads at Scrapfaggot Green, Great Leighs, Essex, England, to widen the road. Psychic havoc broke out. A great boulder was found outside the local pub, chickens were found locked up in rabbit hutches, rabbits were loose in the garden, the church bells chimed irregularly, 30 sheep and two horses were found dead in a field, and a village builder found his scaffold poles tumbled about 'like matchsticks'. The 'Witch's Stone' was replaced and peace was restored.

In 1980 a 30-tonne boulder was removed from the Devil's Marbles to a park in Tennant Creek, an isolated copper mining town in the Australian outback. Aborigines of the Warramungu tribe believe the Marbles are a relic from the 'Dream Time' – when ancestral spirits created the world – and any interference with such relics will lead to sickness and death. After the boulder's removal, a number of Aboriginal children fell ill

rabbi claims he failed to discover Shilo's mother's name.

Even in the calm glade of the Church of England, spiritual contracts are occasionally put out on church thieves. Since the 1970s in Gloucestershire alone, two vicars have performed the commination service: the Reverend Harold Cheales of Wych Rissington in 1973, and the Reverend Robert Nesham of Down Ampney in 1981. The commination service contains 12 curses and leaves room for extemporisation. It first appeared in the 1662 Book of Common Prayer, but in the 1928 revision 'curse' was replaced by 'God's anger and judgement'. It was traditionally used against enemies of the Church on the first day of Lent, or whenever a church or churchyard had been desecrated. Christian curses seem to be, on occasion, just as effective as demonic ones: the old abbeys that Henry VIII seized from the monks after the dissolution of the monasteries in the early 16th century often bedevilled their new owners over generations with the curses laid

By fire and water

Battle Abbey in Sussex (below) was the scene of a grim curse laid on the descendants of Sir Anthony Browne, 'Esquire to the Body of Henry VIII, Master of the Horse and Justice in Eyre', in 1538.

with sores on their legs, and a tribal elder, Mick Taylor, warned that 'someone would get killed' if the stone were not returned. In March 1981 Mick Taylor died from meningitis at the age of 50. The town then agreed to return the boulder.

In late 1981 councillors in King's Lynn, Norfolk, England, refused to move an 18th-century obelisk that was in danger from vandals. A Latin inscription reads: 'Whoever shall remove or have removed this monument let him die the last of his line.'

Rocks of wrath

During the summer of 1977 airline vice-president Ralph Loffert, of Buffalo, New York state, USA, his wife and four children visited the Hawaiian volcano Mauna Loa. While there they collected some stones from the volcano despite a warning from the locals that this would anger the volcano goddess, Pele. Some claim to have seen Pele, who traditionally appears to warn of imminent eruptions. Shortly after they returned home, Mauna Loa erupted. Within a few months one of the Loffert boys, Todd, developed appendicitis, had knee surgery and broke his wrist; another son, Mark, sprained an ankle and broke his arm; another son, Dan, caught an eye infection and had to wear glasses; and the daughter, Rebecca, lost two front teeth in a fall. In July 1978, the Lofferts sent the stones to a friend in Hawaii who was asked to return them to the volcano. But the disasters continued – Mark hurt his knee, Rebecca broke three more teeth, Dan fractured a hand bone, while Todd dislocated an elbow and fractured his wrist again. Mark then confessed that he still had three stones. They were returned – and the trouble ceased.

Mrs Allison Raymond of Ontario, Canada, and her family also took some stones away from the volcano. She told reporters:

According to tradition, Sir Anthony was cursed at the feast held to celebrate his ownership of the abbey by a monk who was angry at the seizure of Church lands during the Reformation.

The curse was specific: the family would die 'by fire or water'. It seems, however, that the curse went awry: Sir Anthony's other property, Cowdray Park – which he had inherited from his half-cousin, the Earl of Southampton – was burned down; but this was much later, in 1793, after the property had passed into the hands of another family.

Antony Hippisley Coxe, compiler of *Haunted Britain* (1974), records that the curse came unstuck yet again, in 1907, when the Duchess of Cleveland – who had rented Battle Abbey briefly – drowned in its grounds on her way to church, but her daughter, who was with her, survived.

Above: a 788-year-old curse is ritually lifted by the Chief Rabbi at the consecration of Clifford's Tower in York on 31 October 1978. On the night of 16 March 1190, 150 Jews fled to the tower where they died by their own hand rather than fall into a mob's hands. The last to die was the Chief Rabbi, whose final act was to curse the city of York. Until well into the 20th century York was avoided by Jews – even though nearby Leeds has always had a thriving Jewish community

Right: 'The curse has come upon me, cried the Lady of Shallott' – Tennyson's doomed heroine prepares to meet her fate

Jon Erickson, a naturalist at the Volcanoes National Park in Hawaii, said he receives up to 40 packages of rock a day from frightened tourists who have returned home.

Lieutenant Commander 'Buster' Crabbe dived with Royal Navy men in 1950 in Tobermory Bay, Isle of Mull, in search of the *Duque de Florencia*, a payship of the Spanish Armada, which had been sunk in 1588 with a reputed 30 million pounds of gold on board. One of the trophies with which he surfaced was a skull that medical experts said had belonged to a North African woman. Crabbe disappeared, some maintain mysteriously, while on an underwater mission near Russian warships in Portsmouth harbour in 1956. The following year a coroner decided that the headless body of a frogman washed up at Chichester, Sussex, was that of Crabbe.

The skull that had been found on the

My husband was killed in a head-on car crash and my mother died of cancer. My younger son was rushed to hospital with a pancreas condition that's slowly getting worse. Then he broke his leg. My daughter's marriage nearly broke up and it was only when I posted the rocks back that our luck improved.

Despite warnings, Nixon Morris, a hardwood dealer from El Paso, Texas, took a Mauna Loa stone home in 1979. After returning home he fell off his roof, lightning struck an aerial and ruined several home appliances, and his wife fell ill with a mysterious infection that left her knee swollen.

Then Morris broke a hip and thigh when he fought with a burglar in their house. The family cat was sleeping under the bonnet of his wife's car when she started the engine and was stripped of its fur down one side. Then Morris's grand-daughter fell and broke her arm in two places.

Morris said he had broken the rock in two and given a piece to a friend, adding: 'He brought the rock back to me after he wrecked four cars in less than two years, and he'd never before had a wreck in his life.' In March 1981 Morris sent the rocks back.

Above: the Devil's Marbles, Australia, a sacred Aboriginal site. In 1980 one of the boulders was removed; Mick Taylor, a tribal elder, warned that the removal would lead to sickness and death.
Several children fell ill – and he died the next year, at the age of 50

Below: the Mauna Loa volcano of Hawaii. In 1977 the Loffert family, on holiday from the USA, picked up some stones from the volcano – despite a warning that this would anger the local deity, the goddess Pele. A series of disasters struck the family, ceasing only when the last stone had been sent back to Hawaii. Other tourists have reported similar runs of bad luck after taking stones away

wreck was kept in the Western Isles Hotel, Tobermory, Scotland, where one day the barman accidentally caused it to fall and break. The same day he crashed his motor scooter and cracked *his* skull. He never returned to the island. The hotel owner, Donald Maclean, stored the skull away in a cupboard. In 1970 Richard Forrester, the new English owner of the hotel, drilled a hole in the skull so that he could hang it up in his cocktail bar:

I was using an ordinary electric drill. The first odd thing that happened was that the metal bit of the drill, after piercing the bone, bent inside at an angle of 45 degrees. I found this surprising but thought nothing more about it. Two hours later I was struck

The curse of the Pharoahs

Archaeologists can be said to be modern grave robbers – and as such seem to have paid the price, for many ancient Egyptian tombs apparently carry curses for any who dare to desecrate them.

According to the American journalist Webb Garrison, Professor S. Resden opened an Egyptian tomb in the 1890s that was thus inscribed: 'Whosoever desecrates the tomb of Prince Sennar will be overtaken by the sands and destroyed.' Resden knew he was doomed, it is said. He left Egypt by ship – and died on board, a victim of suffocation with no discernible cause. Small

amounts of sand were found clutched in his hands.

The poetic neatness of this story is, it must be said, rather suspicious and should perhaps be taken with a pinch of salt – or sand.

But the 'curse of the pharaoh' continues. In September 1979, George LaBrash had a stroke while guarding the Tutankhamun mask (left) in San Francisco. In January 1982 he sued the city authorities for disability pay, claiming that the stroke was a job-related injury caused by the alleged curse on the tomb's desecration. The case was dismissed. Was this in itself a refinement of the curse? Has the curse of the boy king moved into legal circles?

Above: the appalling crash that killed film star Jayne Mansfield on 29 June 1967. This was widely rumoured as being no *accident* – Jayne had been cursed by her former friend, Anton la Vey, head of the Church of Satan

Above right: Lance Sieveking, broadcaster and father of author Paul Sieveking. He demonstrated an unusual immunity to a curse laid by black magician Aleister Crowley by living 30 years longer than the curse allowed

by excruciating pain in the back of the head. I was completely incapacitated for two days. Since then I have been taking prescribed pills but the searing pain continues and never leaves.

And the only other person to handle the skull since the drilling had also experienced searing headaches.

The notion of a curse affecting a whole family is at least as old as civilisation. The ancient Greeks were firm believers in the efficacy of curses – the most celebrated curse affecting the house of Atreus: Atreus killed the son of the god Hermes in a love contest, and Hermes put a curse on the murderer 'and all his house'. Atreus killed his own son by mistake; his grandson, the Homeric hero Agamemnon, was killed by his wife and her lover; and she in turn was murdered by her son and daughter.

In Moorish Spain, a curse was believed to hang over the great Abencerrage family – 'the Flower of Granada'. Many died in war and vendettas before the whole family was wiped out by King Muley Hassan on one of the patios of the Alhambra palace during the 15th century.

Relatively speaking

In Britain, several aristocratic families are believed to be afflicted by family curses. In the 18th century the Scottish Earl of Breadaulbin moved a graveyard to build the castle of Taynmouth. According to tradition a lady whose grave was disturbed laid a curse on the family whereby no two earls of the same line would succeed each other. The prophecy apparently came true.

Even writing about curses might be considered a hazardous business, but this author draws a certain comfort from the apparent immunity of his father. In 1928 the magician Aleister Crowley ('The Beast'), recently expelled from Sicily, met the young radio producer Lance Sieveking in Cassis on the French Riviera. They spent many hours in conversation, and Crowley subsequently

cast Sieveking's horoscope. It contained a number of predictions that were later fulfilled. One, however, was not. Crowley wrote: 'By the way, you will oblige me personally by dying at the age of forty-five.' Sieveking was then 32 but he disobligingly lived to be 75.

Crowley's curses, however, often successfully claimed their victims. The last to go was young Dr William Brown Thompson, who withheld the addicted Beast's supply of morphia. In a rage, Crowley put a curse on him, saying that when he died he would take the doctor with him. And so it came to pass. Crowley died on 1 December 1947, aged 72. Thompson was dead within 24 hours.

EXTRA! BUFFALO EVENING NEWS. EXTRA!

VOL. XLII—NO. 132. BUFFALO, N. Y., FRIDAY, SEPTEMBER 13, 1901. PRICE ONE CENT.

| EXTRA! | EXTRA! | EXTRA! | EXTRA! |

PRESIDENT DEAD!

William McKinley Passed Away at the Milburn Home From Effects of Cowardly Assassin's Bullet.

No hiding place

Bad luck appears to attach itself to some people with a single-mindedness that seems to imply an organising intelligence.

WHILE A CURSE is a conscious invocation of misfortune against others, a jinx is merely a bringer of bad luck – why it starts is anybody's guess. Jinxes may be curses in disguise, unknown to the victims. It could even be that someone who suffers a series of inexplicable misfortunes comes to believe himself to be jinxed – and so unconsciously brings about further disasters.

For 400 years the Haanappel family of Doesburg in Holland have had the palms of their hands turn black six months after they are born. Doctors say this is the result of a gene mutation, but local folklore maintains that a Haanappel saved a church from fire by ringing the bells, burning his hands as he slid down the bell rope. The Devil, in his anger, cursed him and his heirs forever.

No one has come up with an explanation for the misfortunes of the Guinness brewery family. In 1978 they suffered four deaths in as many months: in May Lady Henrietta Guinness plunged to her death from an aqueduct in Spoleto, Italy; in June another Guinness heiress drowned in a bath while trying to inject herself with heroin. Also in June, Major Dennys Guinness was found dead in Hampshire with an empty pill bottle by his side. In August, John Guinness, then an aide to British Prime Minister James Callaghan, survived a head-on collision in Norfolk, but his four-year-old son was killed and another son seriously injured. Lady Henrietta's cousin, Tara Browne, had died in a car crash in Chelsea in 1966.

Jinxes can perform to the most exacting timetables. The Milli family, from a lonely mountain village in central Italy, seem to

Below: the death of 21-year old Tara Browne – heir to the Guinness family fortune – in 1966 was only one tragedy in the long history of the family jinx. Fatal crashes and inexplicable suicides, death plunges and drug accidents have bedevilled the Guinness family

have such a jinx. On 17 January 1949 a woman in the family died, as happened on the same day in 1959 and 1969. On 17 January 1978, misfortune struck a year early when Giuseppina Milli, aged 72, died of a heart attack. On 17 January 1989 the remaining family members plan to stay in hospital, taking no chances.

Black Tuesday

This patterning effect sometimes emerges around specific days of the week as well. The Marquis of Chaumont hated Tuesday so much that he had the word cut out of all his books and papers. He was ill every Tuesday for 79 years and died on a Tuesday in 1780.

One famous periodical jinx hangs over the American presidency. Since 1840 no president elected in a year ending with a zero has survived his term of office. Pneumonia took off William H. Harrison (elected in 1840). Lincoln (1860), Garfield (1880), McKinley (whose second term began in 1900) and Kennedy (1960) were all assassinated while still in office. Harding (1920) had a heart attack; Roosevelt (1940) died of polio. And there has already been one assassination attempt on Reagan (1980).

There is a jinxed aria in Halévy's opera *Charles VI*, which was premiered at the Opéra Comique in Paris in 1852. As the celebrated tenor Maffiani sang 'Oh God, smash him', meaning the traitorous. villain, he lifted his eyes to the ceiling. One of the stage hands immediately toppled to his death from a perch aloft. Maffiani was inconsolable, and the following morning the newspapers were calling it the 'Curse Aria'. On the next night when he sang it he fixed his eyes on an empty box. Suddenly, the curtains of the box parted and a man taking his seat swayed and toppled to his death. On the third night the tenor sang the aria staring at the floor, but a musician in the orchestra pit

One of the most famous periodical jinxes hangs over American presidents who are elected in years ending with a zero. Abraham Lincoln (left, centre), who came to office in 1860, McKinley (left), who was elected in 1900 for the second time, Roosevelt (bottom centre), whose third term as president began in 1940, and John F. Kennedy (below), who was elected in 1960, all died during their terms of office. And there has already been one attempt on the life of Ronald Reagan (bottom), who was elected in 1980

played off-key. Maffiani glared at him and he died of a heart attack.

Further performances were cancelled, but in 1858 Napoleon III asked Halévy to stage *Charles VI* for him. On the night before the performance Napoleon and Eugénie narrowly escaped bombs hurled by Italian revolutionaries. The opera was cancelled and has never been staged since.

Various stretches of railway and road appear to have jinxes on them. The railway line between Acklington and Belford in Northumberland, a distance of 21 miles (34 kilometres), has been dubbed the 'hoodoo line'. Passengers just fall out of 'secure' doors on London to Edinburgh expresses. Two lives were lost within 18 days in August 1980, exactly a year after an identical death fall. A young sailor had also died on the same stretch in 1978. British Rail remain mystified.

A 100-yard (90-metre) section of the M4 motorway between Swindon and Chippenham in Wiltshire claimed four lives within a week in the spring of 1979. Traffic experts could find no obvious cause. Equally baffling were a string of fatal 'carbon-copy' accidents at night on a stretch of the Sevenoaks bypass between Gracious Lane Bridge and Chipstead flyover in Kent. In each case the driver swerved inexplicably across the grass verge separating the two carriageways.

In the first crash in November 1977, three people lost their lives. Then in May 1978 three young men died 100 yards (90 metres) away. In the following August another young man in a car swerved to his death, and in February 1979 a mother and her son heading for Tonbridge were killed when another car left the northbound carriageway and hit them head-on.

Road to dusty death

A possible clue lies in the unnerving experience of Mrs Babs Davidson, an employee of British Telecom. She was driving home in winter moonlight along the jinxed road around the time of the last-mentioned crash. She knew the road well, but suddenly the way ahead was no longer familiar. Part of it was blacked out and a road she had never seen before forked mistily away to her right. 'I felt a tremendous compulsion to take it,' she recalled, 'but forced myself to go on. I was very relieved when I found I had done the right thing and was still heading north on the carriageway.' The appearance of a ghost road could easily be dismissed as an hallucination due to fatigue, but Mrs Davidson claims to have seen it on two subsequent occasions, although she is unable to identify the spot exactly. And usually her claims have been taken seriously by Department of Transport investigators looking for the cause of the crashes.

Many jinxes seem to be analogous to an outbreak of disease that infects a few victims and then peters out. Behavioural syndromes

Left: the jinxed stretch of the Sevenoaks bypass in Kent, between Gracious Lane Bridge and Chipstead flyover, where several fatal 'carbon copy' accidents took place in the late 1970s. One driver who avoided disaster was Mrs Babs Davidson who, on three occasions, claims to have seen a 'ghost' road branching off the main carriageway. She felt an overwhelming urge to follow it, but managed to continue on her route. Had the other drivers succumbed and taken the ghost road – to their deaths?

such as mass faintings and the spread of rumours and panic also seem to fit this pattern.

Films about the occult often seem to engender such an outbreak, their productions plagued with accidents, illness and death. *The omen I* was typical. Star Gregory Peck's aeroplane was struck by lightning, as was one carrying author David Seltzer and Robert Munger, who devised the film. Director Richard Donner had a rough flight too and was later hit by a car. Lightning struck the building next to his Rome hotel. Special effects man John Richardson was in a car accident with a lorry in Holland, and his passenger was killed. When he regained consciousness, he saw a milestone for the town of Ommen. A pack of dogs ran amok and injured two stuntmen, and a zoo keeper was killed by a tiger the day the film crew left the zoo.

Casualties of curses?

We all know, or have read about, accident-prone people. Whether they suffer from some elusive behavioural 'infection' or had a curse put on them at an early age by some ill-disposed person, it is impossible to say. Perhaps someone (or something) 'up there' (or wherever) is trying to get a message through to the hapless victims.

Brian Challender, a bricklayer from Bournemouth, Dorset, was born on a Friday the 13th, which he believes accounts for his run of misfortune. As a boy he had a bad bicycle accident, was knocked out by a golf club and attacked by a man with an axe. He was stabbed at a fairground, pinned down by a 55-tonne motorway earth mover, trapped under a garage door, stunned by falling metal on a building site (he had removed his hard hat in the heat to cool down), scarred for life by steam and rammed by a rowing boat off Bournemouth pier. His last recorded disaster was when he was bending down to pick up a pin for good luck – he was knocked unconscious by a falling brick.

Besides the accident-prone, there are the

'Jonahs', those people who always seem to be around to witness the misfortune of others. A certain Mrs Murray was a passenger on the final journeys of three doomed ships: the *Titanic*, the *Lusitania* and the *Celtic*, which was rammed by the *Anaconda* in 1927. It happens on land too. Dr Max Benis, a specialist in allergies, has been on hand at least 19 times to help people in distress. Wherever he goes people touch live wires, choke on their food, begin to drown or fall off high rocks. Said the *Daily Mail* of 6 December 1977, 'not many of the victims seem particularly grateful to Dr Max.'

Also within this category are people who seem to trigger illness in others in some unfathomable way. The classic example is 'Typhoid Mary', a cook in New York in 1906. Several people contracted typhoid and she was detained in hospital for three years, even though she was not suffering from typhoid herself. After her release she returned to work as a cook under various aliases. About five years later, 25 people in the Sloane Maternity Hospital, New York, went down with the disease and two died. Mary was cooking at the hospital and was detained again.

Below: the *Lusitania*, which sank in 1915. A certain Mrs Murray survived not only the wreck of this ship but also that of the *Titanic*, in 1912, and that of the *Celtic*, in 1927. Jinx, curse – or some kind of *good* luck?

Left: the popular view of the 'crimes' of the Frenchwoman Jeanne Weber, known as 'the Ogress'. Accused of murdering several children in the early 1900s, she was finally acquitted – for it seemed that she was one of those unfortunate people whose mere presence causes the sudden, inexplicable death of others

Below: Wesley MacIntire is carried from the wreck of the Sunshine Skyway Bridge in Florida, USA, which was rammed by a freighter in May 1980 (bottom). He was the sole survivor of this disaster and has emerged unscathed from many others. He devoutly hopes that his life is not being preserved by Providence just for one final accident

encephalitis, an inflammation of the brain. A few days later, another nearly died of meningitis. In February 1981, after Christine had moved to Lakeland, Florida, two young brothers in her care went into convulsions, but recovered after emergency treatment. A few days later, on 23 February, Christine was looking after another boy when he died of myocarditis, an inflammation of the heart muscle. Three days later, the same disease killed another of her charges. Finally, on 14 July 1981, a little girl died in her arms after being inoculated against diphtheria, whooping cough and tetanus. Extensive medical tests showed that Christine was not carrying any communicable diseases. She told the Florida newspaper *Sentinel Star*: 'Sometimes I wonder if I don't have some kind of spell over me when I get around young'uns.'

Another category of jinxed folk are those who constantly emerge unscathed from accidents. The life story of Wesley MacIntire illustrates this rather well. On 9 May 1980 a freighter rammed the Sunshine Skyway Bridge in Florida, USA. Thirty-five people were killed, and the sole survivor was MacIntire, who swam to the surface when his pick-up truck plunged into the river.

During the Second World War when he was in the navy he had dived off the side of his

The case of Jeanne Weber, known throughout France as 'the Ogress', is featured in this author's book *Man bites man* (1981). In 1906 she was accused of murdering two of her children and two of her nephews. The children had died after being alone with her, but the deaths were proved to be natural and she was acquitted. The following year she was staying in the house of a woodcutter when a small child died of convulsions while sitting on her knee. After two further trials she was acquitted.

More recently, four children died and three narrowly escaped death while being watched over by an 18-year-old epileptic, Christine Fallings of Blountstown, Florida, USA. In February 1980, the first died of

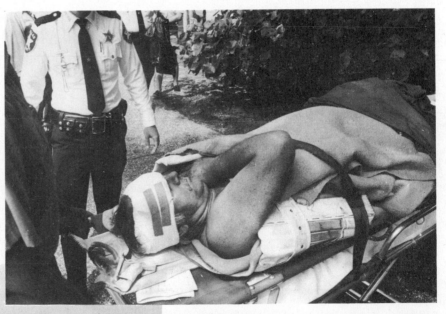

ship seconds before it was bombed. Later, as a lorry driver, he drove a 20-tonne load of gravel $1\frac{1}{2}$ miles (2.5 kilometres) down a mountainside after his brakes failed, and managed to spin the lorry round and round in a parking lot until it stopped. In 1959 he crashed a container lorry loaded with explosive gases. It did not explode. Then an air tank in another lorry he was driving did explode, but MacIntire was saved by his mattress. There were many other accidents that he managed to survive. 'The only thing I can think of,' he said, 'is that the Good Lord must really be saving me up for something. I hope it's not another accident.'

Coincidences and connections

Above: the assassination of King Umberto I of Italy by the anarchist Bresci on 29 July 1900. His death and important events in his life were astonishingly closely paralleled by the life of another Umberto – a restaurant proprietor in a small town in northern Italy

Below: the German philosopher Arthur Schopenhauer (1788–1860), who believed that coincidences were a reflection of the 'wonderful pre-established harmony' of the Universe

Every one of us has, at some time, experienced a coincidence. Mathematicians explain them away as mere chance events – but there are those who seek deeper reasons. PERROTT PHILLIPS investigates

ON THE EVENING OF 28 JULY 1900, King Umberto I of Italy dined with his aide in a restaurant in Monza, where he was due to attend an athletics meeting the next day. With astonishment, he noticed that the proprietor looked exactly like him and, speaking to him, he discovered that there were other similarities.

The restaurateur was also called Umberto; like the King, he had been born in Turin – and on the same day; and he had married a girl called Margherita on the day the King married his Queen Margherita. And he had opened his restaurant on the day that Umberto I was crowned King of Italy.

The King was intrigued, and invited his double to attend the athletics meeting with him. But next day at the stadium the King's aide informed him that the restaurateur had died that morning in a mysterious shooting accident. And even as the King expressed his regret, he himself was shot dead by an anarchist in the crowd.

Another strange coincidence connected with a death occurred much more recently. On Sunday 6 August 1978 the little alarm clock that Pope Paul VI had bought in 1923 – and that for 55 years had woken him at six every morning – rang suddenly and shrilly. But it was not six o'clock: the time was 9.40 p.m. and, for no explicable reason, the clock started ringing as the Pope lay dying. Later, Father Romeo Panciroli, a Vatican spokesman, commented, 'It was most strange. The

These foolish things...

The most striking coincidences often involve the most commonplace of objects or occasions, like the bizarre experience related by the Chicago newspaper columnist Irv Kupcinet (left):

'I had just checked into the Savoy Hotel in London. Opening a drawer in my room, I found, to my astonishment, that it contained some personal things belonging to a friend of mine, Harry Hannin, then with the Harlem Globetrotters basketball team.

'Two days later, I received a letter from Harry, posted in the Hotel Meurice, in Paris, which began "You'll never believe this." Apparently, Harry had opened a drawer in *his* room and found a tie with my name on it. It was a room I had stayed in a few months earlier.'

The Renaissance philosopher Pico della Mirandola, one of a long line of thinkers, starting with Hippocrates, the 'father of medicine', who believed that the world was governed by a principle of wholeness – and that coincidences could be explained as like events seeking each other out

Pope was very fond of the clock. He bought it in Poland and always took it with him on his trips.'

Every one of us has experienced a coincidence – however trivial – at some time or other. But some of the extreme examples seem to defy all logic, luck or reason.

Powers of the Universe

It is not surprising, therefore, that the 'theory of coincidence' has excited scientists, philosophers and mathematicians for more than 2000 years. Running like a thread through all their theories and speculations is one theme: what are coincidences about? Do they have a hidden message for us? What unknown force do they represent? Only in this century have any real answers been suggested, answers that strike at the very roots of established science and prompt the question: are there powers in the Universe of which we are still only dimly aware?

Early cosmologists believed that the world was held together by a kind of principle of

wholeness. Hippocrates, known as the father of medicine, who lived at some time between 460 and 375 BC, believed the Universe was joined together by 'hidden affinities' and wrote: 'There is one common flow, one common breathing, all things are in sympathy.' According to this theory, coincidence could be explained by 'sympathetic' elements seeking each other out.

The Renaissance philosopher Pico della Mirandola wrote in 1557: 'Firstly, there is a unity in things whereby each thing is at one with itself. Secondly, there is the unity whereby one creature is united with the others and all parts of the world constitute one world.'

This belief has continued, in a barely altered form, in much more modern times. The philosopher Arthur Schopenhauer (1788–1860) defined coincidence as 'the simultaneous occurrence of causally unconnected events.' He went on to suggest that simultaneous events ran in parallel lines and the selfsame event, although a link in

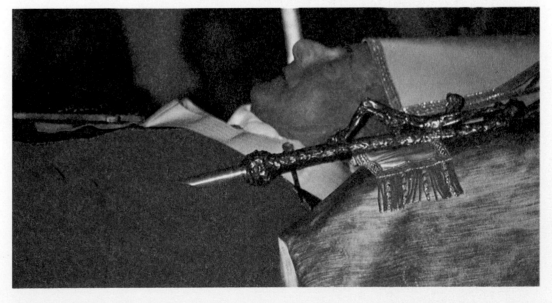

The lying-in-state of Pope Paul VI. At 9.40 p.m. on 6 August 1978, as the Pope lay dying, his bedside alarm clock – set for six in the morning – inexplicably began to ring

totally different chains, nevertheless falls into place in both, so that the fate of one individual invariably fits the fate of another, and each is the hero of his own drama while simultaneously figuring in a drama foreign to him. This is something that surpasses our powers of comprehension and can only be conceived as possible by the virtue of the most wonderful pre-established harmony. Everyone must participate in it. Thus everything is interrelated and mutually attuned.

Probing the future

The idea of a 'collective unconscious' – an underground storehouse of memories through which minds can communicate – has been debated by several thinkers. One of the more extreme theories to explain coincidence was put forward by the British mathematician Adrian Dobbs in the 1960s. He coined the word 'psitron' to describe an unknown force that probed, like radar, a second time dimension that was probabilistic rather than deterministic. The psitron absorbed future probabilities and relayed them back to the present, bypassing the normal human senses and somehow conveying the information directly to the brain.

The first person to study the laws of coincidence scientifically was Dr Paul Kammerer, Director of the Institute of Experimental Biology in Vienna. From the age of 20, he started to keep a 'logbook' of coincidences. Many were essentially trivial: people's names that kept cropping up in separate conversations, successive concert or cloakroom tickets with the same number, a phrase in a book that kept recurring in real life. For hours, Kammerer sat on park

Dr Paul Kammerer who, in 1919, published the first systematic study of coincidence

benches recording the people who wandered past, noting their sex, age, dress, whether they carried walking sticks or umbrellas. After making the necessary allowances for things like rush-hour, weather and time of year, he found the results broke down into 'clusters of numbers' of a kind familiar to statisticians, gamblers, insurance companies and opinion pollsters.

Kammerer called the phenomenon 'seriality', and in 1919 he published his conclusions in a book called *Das Gesetz der Serie* (The law of seriality). Coincidences, he claimed, came in series – or 'a recurrence or clustering in time or space whereby the individual numbers in the sequence are not connected by the same active cause.'

Coincidence, suggested Kammerer, was merely the tip of an iceberg in a larger cosmic principle that mankind, as yet, hardly recognises.

Like gravity, it is a mystery; but unlike gravity, it acts selectively to bring together in space and time things that possess some affinity. 'We thus arrive,' he concluded, 'at the image of a world mosaic or cosmic kaleidoscope, which, in spite of constant shufflings and rearrangements, also takes care of bringing like and like together.'

The great leap forward happened 50 years later, when two of Europe's most brilliant minds collaborated to produce the most searching book on the powers of coincidence – one that was to provoke both controversy and attack from rival theorists.

The two men were Wolfgang Pauli – whose daringly conceived exclusion principle earned him the Nobel Prize for Physics – and the Swiss psychologist-philosopher, Professor Carl Gustav Jung. Their treatise bore the unexciting title: *Synchronicity, an*

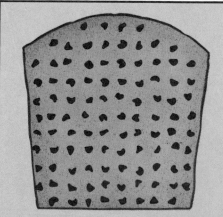

The cluster effect

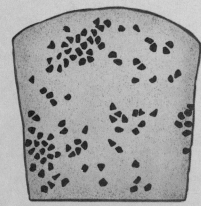

In his book *Homo Faber* Max Frisch tells the extraordinary story of a man who, through a series of coincidences, meets the daughter he never knew he had, falls in love with her and sets in motion a train of events that results in her death. But Faber, a rational man, refuses to see anything more than the laws of chance in his story:

'I don't deny that it was more than a coincidence which made things turn out as they did, it was a whole series of coincidences. . . . The occasional occurrence of the improbable does not imply the intervention of a higher power. . . . The term probability includes improbability at the extreme limits of probability, and when the improbable does occur this is no cause for surprise, bewilderment or mystification.'

Few people could be so matter-of-fact in the face of the events Frisch describes – but Faber may be right. Every mathematician knows that a random distribution of events produces – surprisingly – a clustering effect, just as cherries randomly distributed in a cake will tend to be found in groups (left) rather than in the orderly arrangement one might expect (far left). The mathematician is not surprised by coincidences, or clusters of random events – but neither can he predict them!

Above: Wolfgang Pauli (1900–1958), the Nobel prize-winning physicist who, together with the eminent psychologist C.G. Jung, introduced the concept of *synchronicity* to help explain the occurrence of coincidences

Right: the decorated dome of the mosque of Madresh, Isfahan, Iran. The pattern represents the eternal pilgrimage of the soul – it unrolls in a continuous thread like the breath of the Universe, by which all things are connected. Modern physics suggests that this idea of 'interconnectedness' may be of use in providing non-causal explanations of events that are now dismissed as coincidence

acausal connecting principle. Described by one American reviewer as 'the paranormal equivalent of a nuclear explosion', it used the term 'synchronicity' to extend Kammerer's theory of seriality.

Order out of chaos

According to Pauli, coincidences were 'the visible traces of untraceable principles'. Coincidences, elaborated Jung, whether they come singly or in series, are manifestations of a barely understood universal principle that operates quite independently of the known laws of physics. Interpreters of the Pauli-Jung theory have concluded that telepathy, precognition and coincidences themselves are all manifestations of a single mysterious force at work in the Universe that is trying to impose its own kind of discipline on the utter confusion of human life.

Of all contemporary thinkers, none has written more extensively about the theory of coincidence than Arthur Koestler, who sums up the phenomenon in the vivid phrase 'puns of destiny'.

One particularly striking 'pun' was related

Above: Arthur Koestler, a science journalist who has written extensively about the search for a scientific explanation of coincidence – and its philosophical implications. It was he who coined the apt phrase 'puns of destiny' to describe the phenomenon

to Koestler by a 12-year-old English school-boy named Nigel Parker:

Many years ago, the American horror-story writer, Edgar Allan Poe, wrote a book called *The narrative of Arthur Gordon Pym.* In it, Mr Pym was travelling in a ship that wrecked. The four survivors were in an open boat for many days before they decided to kill and eat the cabin boy whose name was Richard Parker.

Some years *later*, in the summer of 1884, my great-grandfather's cousin was cabin boy in the yawl *Mignonette* when she foundered, and the four survivors were in an open boat for many days. Eventually, the three senior members of the crew killed and ate the cabin boy. His name was Richard Parker.

Such strange and seemingly meaningful incidents abound – can there really be no more to them than mere coincidence?

Against all the odds

It is a curious fact that the most striking coincidences often involve the most trivial of events. If, as many people believe, coincidences have some inner meaning, why are they apparently so pointless?

THE BRITISH ACTOR Anthony Hopkins was delighted to hear he had landed a leading role in a film based on the book *The girl from Petrovka* by George Feifer. A few days after signing the contract, Hopkins travelled to London to buy a copy of the book. He tried several bookshops, but there wasn't one to be had. Waiting at Leicester Square underground station for his train home, he noticed a book lying apparently discarded on a bench. Incredibly, it was *The girl from Petrovka*. That in itself would have been coincidence enough, but in fact it was merely the beginning of an extraordinary chain of events. Two years later, in the middle of filming in Vienna, Hopkins was visited by George Feifer, the author. Feifer mentioned that he did not have a copy of his own book. He had lent the last one – containing his own annotations – to a friend who had lost it somewhere in London. With mounting astonishment, Hopkins handed Feifer the book he had found. 'Is this the one?' he asked, 'with the notes scribbled in the margins?' It was the same book.

Dr Paul Kammerer, the former Director of the Institute of Experimental Biology in Vienna – and one of the first men to try to define the 'laws of coincidence' – would have relished that example. He was particularly fond of literary coincidences, and there are several in his book *Das Gesetz der Serie* ('The law of seriality'), published in 1919, which introduced the theory of 'seriality'.

Kammerer's work was also too early to include another literary coincidence, which was experienced by Dame Rebecca West, the novelist and historian. She found herself at a dead end when she went to the Royal Institute of International Affairs to research a specific episode in the Nuremberg trials:

I looked up the Trials in the library and was horrified to find they were published in a form almost useless to the researcher. After hours of search, I went along the line of shelves to an assistant librarian and said, 'I can't find it, there's no clue, it could be *any* of

British actor Anthony Hopkins (right) found himself caught up in an extraordinary sequence of events when he picked up a book in an underground station in London. Amazingly, it was *The girl from Petrovka* by George Feifer (below), whose film version he was to star in – and it was Feifer's own copy

Bottom: Dame Rebecca West, who experienced a classic case of both 'literary' and 'helpful' coincidence when she had come to a dead end in her research

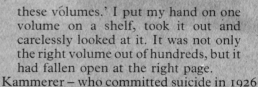

these volumes.' I put my hand on one volume on a shelf, took it out and carelessly looked at it. It was not only the right volume out of hundreds, but it had fallen open at the right page.

Kammerer – who committed suicide in 1926 – suggested that coincidences occurred in series or clusters and defined 'seriality' as 'a recurrence of the same or similar things or events in time or space.' Seriality, he concluded, 'is ubiquitous and continuous in life, nature and cosmos. It is the umbilical cord that connects thought, feeling, science and art with the womb of the universe which gave birth to them.'

Thirty years later, the Nobel prize-winning physicist Wolfgang Pauli and the philosopher-psychologist Professor Carl

Gustav Jung extended Kammerer's work with their theory of 'synchronicity'. Jung defined the word as 'the simultaneous occurrence of two meaningful but not causally connected events . . . a coincidence in time of two or more causally unrelated events which have the same or similar meaning.'

Although approaching the theory of coincidences from different directions, all three men hinted at a mysterious and barely understood force at work in the Universe, a force that was trying to impose its own kind of order on the chaos of human life.

If this seems fanciful, one of the most prolific of all contemporary thinkers on the subject, Arthur Koestler, points out that current biological – as well as physical – research strongly suggests a basic tendency of nature to create order out of disorder.

Not surprisingly, sceptics reject these theories. They explain coincidence in terms of the laws of probability: if something *can* happen then, however small the probability of the event, you should not be too surprised if it eventually *does* happen. A classic example is that a monkey at a typewriter, pressing the keys at random, will eventually – 'as time tends to infinity', as the mathematicians say – type out the entire works of Shakespeare. As science writer Martin Gardner puts it, 'Trillions of events, large and trivial, happen to billions of human beings every day. Therefore, it is inevitable that surprising things occur now and again.'

Another example is the unlikely chance of a bridge player being dealt all 13 cards of one suit. The odds are something like 635 billion to one. Yet, according to probability theory, if enough bridge hands are dealt, it will eventually happen. And indeed it did. Vera Nettick, of Princeton, New Jersey, found herself holding all 13 diamonds. She bid a grand slam and had the memorable experience of being able to lay her incredible hand down on the table.

The followers of seriality and synchronicity – and their later developments – think otherwise. Dealing cards and spinning coins are one thing, they claim. But bizarre coincidences that throw together people or events represent an entirely different force at work.

In his early researches, Kammerer classified coincidences – and he had collected hundreds of examples, often quite trivial, to support his theories – into various types. These mainly depended on the order in which they occurred, the number of parallel coincidences, whether they related to names numbers or situations, and the elements they had in common.

Modern research now divides coincidences into two main categories, the trivial – like the incredible bridge hand – and the significant. Significant coincidences are subdivided into clearly recognisable types: the literary coincidence (like Dame Rebecca West's experience in the library), warning coincidences, useful coincidences (where the right thing happens at the right time), it's-a-small-world coincidences (bringing people together when least expected) and conjuring coincidences, incidents that are like examples of psychic sleight-of-hand.

Nazis in Fleet Street?

There are classic examples in each category, but the quintessential literary coincidence happened just before the Allied invasion of Europe in 1944.

Every aspect of the huge campaign – to drive out the Nazis and end the Second World War – was top secret and referred to only by codewords. The operation itself was known as OVERLORD. The naval spearhead was disguised by the name NEPTUNE. The two French beaches where the landing was to take place were coded UTAH and OMAHA. And the artificial harbours to be used to supply the troops at the beach-head were known as MULBERRY.

Incredibly, in the 33 days before D-Day, 6 June, each of these secret words appeared as the answer to a clue in the London *Daily*

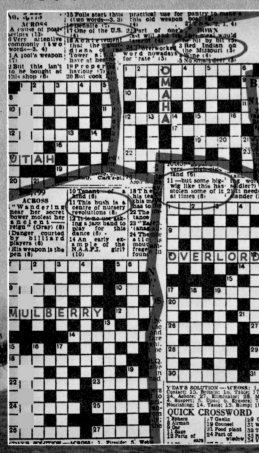

Left: by an amazing coincidence, many of the key code-words used in the strategic planning of the Allied invasion of Europe in 1944 – OVERLORD, NEPTUNE, MULBERRY, UTAH, OMAHA – appeared as solutions to *Daily Telegraph* crossword clues in the weeks before D-Day. Security men quickly checked the *Telegraph* offices – but found no Nazi spy, only schoolmaster Leonard Dawe, who had been compiling the crossword for 20 years

Telegraph crossword. The key word OVER-LORD appeared only four days before the landing.

Security men immediately descended on the Fleet Street offices of the *Telegraph*, expecting to bag a Nazi spy. Instead, they found schoolmaster Leonard Dawe, who had been harmlessly compiling the paper's crossword for 20 years. Dawe was flabbergasted, and took a long time to convince them that he had been totally ignorant of the significance of the words.

The clairvoyant photograph

For an extraordinary conjuring coincidence, however, one can do no better than listen to the curious, and strangely inconsequential, experience of Mrs Eileen Bithell, of Portsmouth, Hampshire.

'For more than 20 years, a framed sign saying Closed on Wednesdays hung in the window of my parents' grocery shop. A few days before my brother's wedding, the sign was taken down to be altered. When we removed it from the frame, we discovered to our surprise that the sign had been painted on the back of a photograph. There was an even bigger surprise. The picture showed my brother's bride-to-be as a small girl, in the

Top: a game of bridge in progress. Card games provide the opportunity for the most spectacular, if trivial, of coincidences

Above: Sir James Jeans (1877–1946), the eminent physicist who remarked that science shows that the Universe looks more like 'a great thought than a great machine'

arms of his future father-in-law.

'Nobody knows how this particular photograph came to be used as the shop sign. For none of the people were known to my family at the time the sign was put up. Yet now, 20 years later, our two families were to be joined in marriage.'

Coincidences like these support the view of Sir James Jeans, the British scientist who died in 1946, who once commented, 'the stream of knowledge is heading towards a non-mechanical reality; the universe begins to look more like a great thought than a great machine' – or, as Eddington put it, 'The stuff of the world is mind-stuff.'

The rational and the occult

In his book *The challenge of chance*, Arthur Koestler suggested that coincidences 'can at least serve as pointers towards a single major mystery – the spontaneous emergence of order out of randomness, and the philosophical challenge implied in that concept. And if that sounds too rational or too occult, collecting coincidences still remains an amusing parlour game.'

Some coincidences start slowly and seem to gain momentum as one improbability follows another. One to cap any 'parlour game' was recounted by a former Fleet Street editor, now a distinguished author. For reasons that will become obvious, all the names have been changed; here is the story:

'Around 12 years ago, when I was editor of a weekly magazine in London, I met and fell in love with a Fleet Street woman journalist named Jackie. Some time afterwards, I parted company with the magazine after a difference of opinion and immediately went, with Jackie, on a Press trip to Capri. What I *didn't* know was that, in the meantime, the girl had met someone else. She had joined a Press party aboard a Swedish ship and had fallen in love with Egon, the shipping line's PRO [public relations officer].

'Six years elapsed in which everyone changed places. Jackie and I split up. She married Egon. He eventually broke with the shipping line. They got a new PRO, a girl named Jan. And Harry was appointed editor of the magazine.

'Then, like some supernatural "action replay", it all started happening again. Harry had an almost identical difference of opinion with the management and left. He immediately went on a previously-arranged Press facility trip . . . to Capri. Who should be on the same trip – again – but Jackie. The man in charge of the visit was her husband, Egon. Meanwhile, I was on the same Swedish ship on which Jackie and Egon had first met and had been introduced to his successor, Jan, who was completely unaware of the earlier relationships. We are now married. And all five of us live in the same area.'

Strange tricks of fate

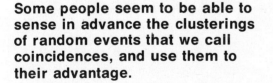

Some people seem to be able to sense in advance the clusterings of random events that we call coincidences, and use them to their advantage.

IT WAS ONLY WHEN his train steamed into Louisville station that George D. Bryson decided to break his trip to New York and visit the historic Kentucky town. He had never been there before and he had to ask where to find the best hotel. Nobody knew he was in Louisville, and, as a joke, he asked the desk clerk at the Brown Hotel, 'Any mail for me?' He was astonished when the clerk handed over a letter addressed to him and bearing his room number. The previous occupant of Room 307 had been another, and entirely different, George D. Bryson.

A remarkable coincidence, by any standards, but made particularly piquant by the fact that the man who tells it most frequently is Dr Warren Weaver, the American mathematician and expert on probabilities, who believes in the theory that coincidences are governed by the laws of chance, and rejects any suggestion of the uncanny or paranormal in coincidences.

On the opposite side of the fence are those who follow the 'seriality' or 'synchronicity'

In 1891 an unknown Englishman named Charles Wells became an overnight sensation as *The man that broke the bank at Monte Carlo*, as a music-hall song later called him. Using no apparent system, he three times 'broke' the 100,000-franc 'bank' allocated to his roulette table at the famous Monte Carlo casino (seen as it is today, above left; in a contemporary drawing from the *Illustrated London News*, above right). Can coincidence explain how Wells was somehow able to sense the winning numbers? We shall never know; after winning for the third time, Wells disappeared, taking his secret with him. He was never seen again

theories of Dr Paul Kammerer, Wolfgang Pauli, and Carl Gustav Jung.

Although the three men approached the theory of coincidences from different directions, their conclusions all hinted at a mysterious and barely understood force at work in the Universe, a force that was trying to impose its own kind of order on the chaos of our world. Modern scientific research, particularly in the fields of biology and physics, also seems to suggest a basic tendency of nature to create order out of chaos.

The sceptics, however, stand firm. When events are happening at random, they argue, you are bound to encounter the clusterings we call 'coincidence'. It is even possible to predict such clusterings or, at least, to predict the frequency with which they are likely to happen.

If you toss a coin many times, the laws of probability dictate that you will end up with an almost equal number of heads and tails. However, the heads and tails will not alternate. There will be runs of one and runs of the other. Dr Weaver calculates that, if you toss a coin 1024 times, for instance, it is likely that there will be one run of eight tails in a row, two of seven in a row, four of six in a row and eight runs of five in a row.

The same is true of roulette. 'Evens' once came up 28 times in succession at Monte Carlo casino. The odds against this happening are around 268 million to one. Yet the randomness experts claim that, as it *could* happen, it did happen – and will happen again somewhere in the world if enough roulette wheels keep spinning long enough.

Mathematicians use this law, for example, to explain the fantastic series of winning numbers that earned Charles Wells the title – in song – of *The man that broke the bank at Monte Carlo*.

Wells – a fat and slightly sinister Englishman – became the subject of the popular music-hall ditty in 1891, when he broke the bank at the Monte Carlo casino three times. He used no apparent system, but put even money bets on red and black, winning nearly every time until he finally exceeded the 100,000 francs 'bank' allocated to each table. On each occasion, attendants lugubriously covered the table with a black 'mourning' cloth and closed it for the rest of the day. The third and last time Wells appeared at the casino, he placed his opening bet on number five, at odds of 35 to 1. He won. He left his original bet and added his winnings to it. Five came up again. This happened five times in succession. Out came the black

Above: Dr Warren Weaver, the American mathematician and probability expert whose study of coincidence has led him to oppose any suggestion that a paranormal force is involved

When a commuter train plunged from an open drawbridge into Newark Bay in New York (below), over 30 people lost their lives. By an ironic coincidence, this tragic incident won many New Yorkers large sums of money. A newspaper picture of the accident (left) showed the number 932 on the rear coach of the train, and many people, sensing some meaning in the number, put their money on it in the Manhattan numbers game – and won

cloth. And out went Wells with his winnings, never to be seen there again.

The seriality and synchronicity theorists – and those who have extended the work of Kammerer, Pauli and Jung – accept the idea of 'clusters' of numbers. But they see 'luck' and 'coincidence' as two sides of the same coin. The classic paranormal concepts of ESP, telepathy and precognition – recurring elements in coincidences – might offer an alternative explanation of why some people are 'luckier' than others.

Modern research breaks coincidences down into two distinct types: trivial (like spinning coins, runs of numbers and amazing hands of cards) and significant. Significant coincidences are those that shuffle together people, events, space and time – past, present and future – in a manner that seems to cross the delicate borderline into the doubtful region of the paranormal.

Macabre significance

Sometimes a coincidence occurs that seems to link, almost capriciously, the rival theories. After a New York commuter train plunged into Newark Bay – killing many passengers – work started on recovering the coaches from the water. One front-page newspaper picture showed the rear coach being winched up, with the number 932 clearly visible on its side. That day, the number 932 came up in the Manhattan numbers game, winning hundreds of thousands of dollars for the hordes of people who – sensing an occult significance in the number – had put their money on it.

Modern researchers now divide significant coincidences into several categories. One is the warning coincidence, with its presentiment of danger or disaster.

Warning coincidences often have an extraordinarily long reach, which is why many

are ignored or go unrecognised. That was certainly the case with three ships, the *Titan*, the *Titanic* and the *Titanian*. In 1898, the American writer Morgan Robertson published a novel about a giant liner, the *Titan*, which sank one freezing April night in the Atlantic after hitting an iceberg on her maiden voyage.

Fourteen years later – in one of the world's worst sea disasters – the *Titanic* sank on a freezing April night in the Atlantic after hitting an iceberg on *her* maiden voyage.

The coincidences did not end there. The ships, both fact and fiction, were around the same tonnage and both disasters occurred in the same stretch of the ocean. Both liners were regarded as 'unsinkable', and neither carried sufficient lifeboats.

Coincidence and premonition

With the extraordinary story of the *Titanian*, the *Titan-Titanic* coincidences begin to defy human belief. On watch one night in April 1935 – during the *Titanian*'s coal-run from the Tyne to Canada – crewman William Reeves began to feel a strong sense of foreboding. By the time the *Titanian* reached the spot where the two other ships had gone down, the feeling was overpowering. Could Reeves stop the ship merely because of a premonition? One thing – a *further* coincidence – made the decision for him. He had been born on the day of the *Titanic* disaster. 'Danger ahead!' he bellowed to the bridge. The words were barely out of his mouth when an iceberg loomed out of the darkness. The ship avoided it just in time.

Another category is the 'it's-a-small-world coincidence', which brings together people and places when least expected – a phenomenon vouched for by Arthur Butterworth, of Skipton, Yorkshire.

During the Second World War, while serving in the army, he ordered a secondhand book on music from a London bookseller. The book eventually reached him at his camp

Coincidence links the fates of the *Titanian* (above) and the famous *Titanic*. Both hit icebergs in the same waters; but the *Titanian* survived

Below: Charles Coghlan, whose dead body made an immense sea journey before being cast up on the shore of his home town

– disguised by the usual military postcode – in the grounds of Taverham Hall, near Norwich. Standing at the window of his army hut, he opened the parcel and, as he did so, a picture postcard – presumably used as a bookmark – fell out. The writing on one side showed the postcard had been written on 4 August 1913. To his astonishment, when he turned it over, the picture showed 'the exact view I had from my hut window at that very moment . . . Taverham Hall.'

If coincidence can reach so easily across time and space in its quest for 'order out of chaos', it is not surprising that it can stretch beyond the grave, too.

While on a tour of Texas in 1899, the Canadian actor Charles Francis Coghlan was taken ill in Galveston and died. It was too far to return his remains to his home on Prince Edward Island, in the Gulf of St Lawrence – more than 3500 miles (5600 kilometres) away by the sea-route – and he was buried in a lead coffin inside a granite vault. His bones had rested less than a year when the great hurricane of September 1900 hit Galveston Island, flooding the cemetery. The vault was shattered and Coghlan's coffin floated out into the Gulf of Mexico. Slowly, it drifted along the Florida coastline and into the Atlantic, where the Gulf Stream picked it up and carried it northwards.

Eight years passed. Then, one day in October 1908, some fishermen on Prince Edward Island spotted a long, weather-scarred box floating near the shore. Coghlan's body had come home. With respect mingled with awe, his fellow islanders buried the actor in the nearby church where he had been christened as a baby.

Chance? Destiny? A mere trick of 'randomness'? Or that strange and powerful force, striving to make sense of the Universe, that some call coincidence?

The meaning of coincidence

Are coincidences merely random events, as mathematicians would have us believe – or is there much more to them? DOUGLAS HILL explores the extraordinary theory developed by the famous psychologist C.G. Jung

'COINCIDENCE' IS A WORD that is often levelled by rationalists at anyone who presumes to suggest that evidence exists for paranormal phenomena. But in recent years defenders of the paranormal have found their own weapon in the concept of 'synchronicity' developed by the great psychologist and philosopher Carl Gustav Jung.

For Jung, a tireless champion of openmindedness, calling an event 'coincidence' did not automatically shut the door on any further examination of the facts. Coincidences happen – fact. Further and more important, coincidences often seem to have *meaning* to the percipients – also an established fact. Jung pointed out that there can be few people who have not had some experience in their lives that they recognise as 'meaningful coincidence'. Many of us may be reluctant to try to explain or evaluate these events for fear of being accused of credulity or superstition. But at the same time we often feel that there is more to them than mere chance.

In his essay on synchronicity, subtitled *An acausal connecting principle*, Jung bravely ventures into this unexplored area (which he describes as 'dark, dubious and hedged about with prejudice'). He reminds us that the natural laws by which we live are based on the principle of *causality*: if this happens, that follows. Empirical observation and experiment prove that this is so, every time. But, Jung insists, there are *facts* that the old principle of causality cannot explain.

Below: Professor J. B. Rhine, the American pioneer ESP researcher whose work was cited by Jung as objective evidence for the existence of an active force behind coincidence

Jung's study of coincidence was stimulated by his own experiences. One extraordinary case involved a golden scarab (below), Egyptian symbol of rebirth, and its European relative, the rose scarab (right)

He cites evidence from the many well-authenticated phenomena gathered by psychical researchers – material on ESP collected by Dr J.B. Rhine, verified cases of precognitive or clairvoyant dreams, and the 'meaningful coincidences' chronicled by researchers such as Dr Paul Kammerer.

Jung was drawn to this mass of material by an intriguing sense that it might contribute in a major way to a greater understanding of the human psyche. In his pioneering essay on synchronicity he is concerned to 'open the field', in the hope that a more thorough and comprehensive tilling will come later. And he is doubtless right to think that his work will inspire later researchers – his preliminary thoughts are breathtaking, for anyone who can overcome prejudice.

Jung is at pains to emphasise what he sees as the true significance of many synchronistic events (his term for meaningful coincidences or 'symbolic parallels'), in which he sees a stirring or 'constellating' of *archetypes* – those immensely powerful motifs that seem to underlie human consciousness. He offers several examples of constellation from his own experience, including the case of a patient whose rationalist preconceptions had set up rigid barriers against the progress of her analysis. She was relating a dream to Jung that involved a golden scarab – a particularly potent symbol of regeneration,

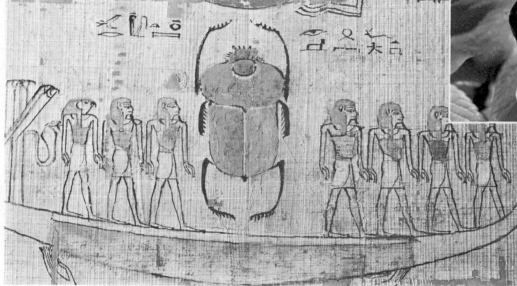

especially in ancient Egypt. As she spoke, an insect flew in at the window – and, with astonishment Jung identified it as one of a species that is the closest thing to a scarab beetle that can be found in Europe. Since 'rebirth' is one way of expressing the transformation that is the goal of Jungian psychotherapy – and since this oddly resonant reinforcing of the rebirth archetype led to a breakthrough for Jung's patient – it is clear how important meaningful coincidence can be.

But isolated phenomena, however remarkable, do not help to build up a workable hypothesis, and Jung went looking for empirical material. He was well aware that he was looking in areas where the scientific establishment said such material did not exist – but then, he points out wryly, so was Galileo. In fact, he chose to examine a body of traditional processes where the idea of synchronicity is taken for granted – that is, the forms of divination that are essentially techniques designed to interpret the meanings of coincidence.

Chinese horoscopes

First he examined the *I Ching*, that ancient Chinese means of summoning our 'intuitive' faculties to aid, or even supplant, our reason in making judgements. From there he turned to traditional astrology, where he put aside the dubious and subjective 'analysis' of character traits and focused instead on a 'harder' connection: the planetary aspects,

The promising Hollywood actor James Dean (right) was killed in a tragic motoring accident in September 1955. Afterwards when the wreck (above) was towed to a garage, the engine slipped and fell onto a mechanic, breaking both his legs. The engine was bought by a doctor, who put it into a racing car and was killed shortly afterwards. In the same race, another driver was killed in a car with the drive shaft from Dean's car. Dean's car was later repaired – and a fire broke out at the garage. It was displayed in Sacramento, and fell of its mount, breaking a teenager's hip. Then, in Oregon, the truck on which the car was mounted slipped and smashed into a shop front. Finally, in 1959, it broke into 11 pieces while sitting on stationary steel supports

Below: a diagram invented by Jung and Pauli to explain their idea that acausility may be a ruling principle of the Universe

especially conjunction of Sun and Moon, long associated by astrologers with marriage. And his empirical search turned up an interestingly high percentage of married couples whose horoscopes *did* show the aspects in question.

Jung would have been very interested in the recent work of the young French statistician Michel Gauquelin, who has sought – and found – correlations between people's professions and the presence in their horoscopes of certain astrological elements.

Perhaps inevitably, however, this aspect of Jung's research has been the one that has attracted the most censure from those who wish to discredit him. People – mostly journalists – who have never read a word of Jung's own voluminous writings are now firmly convinced that he was a credulous crank, or a charlatan, because he 'believed' in astrology, alchemy and other weird subjects. But in fact Jung's own conclusions were that, while he accepted that the results of his experiment were not statistically valid – and that, even if they were, they would not prove the validity of astrology – they did provide him with a set of data concerning the phenomenon of synchronicity.

From his observations Jung draws some conclusions about synchronicity

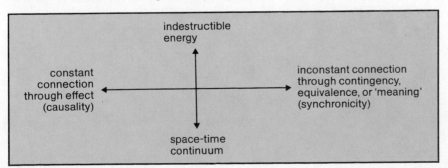

indestructible
energy

constant
connection
through effect
(causality)

inconstant connection
through contingency,
equivalence, or 'meaning'
(synchronicity)

space-time
continuum

and the crucial role that the human psyche plays in it. Coincidences may be purely random events but, as Jung points out, as soon as they seem to carry some symbolic meaning they cease to be random as far as the person involved is concerned. He even considers the idea that the psyche may somehow be operating on external reality to 'cause' coincidences – or that, as in precognitive dreams, the external phenomena are somehow 'transmitted' to the psyche. But he quickly concludes that, because such ideas involve a suspension of our known 'laws' of space and time, we are not capable of ascertaining whether these hypotheses are relevant. And so he comes back to his own theory of an 'acausal' connecting principle governing certain chains of events.

In the face of a meaningful coincidence, Jung says, we can respond in any one of three ways. We can call it 'mere random chance', and turn away with our minds clamped shut; we can call it magic – or telepathy or telekinesis – which is not a great deal more helpful or informative. Or we can postulate the existence of a principle of acausality, and use this idea to investigate the phenomenon more thoroughly.

In the course of doing this Jung puts forward the unsettling thought that space and time may have no real objective existence. They may be only concepts created by the psyche in the course of empirical science's attempts to make rational, measurable sense of the Universe. It is certainly true

A 19th-century Chinese porcelain dish showing the eight trigrams, or symbols of the primary subdivisions of creation; the symbol in the middle represents the positive and negative forces in life, *yang* and *yin*. These concepts were central to the *I Ching*, a Chinese method of divination studied by Jung in his research into coincidences

that these concepts have little true meaning in the systems of thought of many primitive tribes. And, as many leading Jungians have pointed out, a great deal of damage has been done to conventional ideas of space and time by post-Einsteinian advances in particle physics, where so often causality vanishes and probability rules. So, if space and time are merely mental concepts, it is quite reasonable to suppose that they will be capable of being 'conditioned' by the psyche.

Using this hypothesis, Jung goes on to pose a fascinating question. He assumes that, when a meaningful coincidence happens, an image – perhaps from the unconscious – comes into consciousness, and an 'outer' objective phenomenon coincides with it. The psyche perceives meaning in this juxtaposition of events. But what if the meaning could also exist *outside* the psyche? What if meaning exists within the phenomenon itself – just as causality exists, demonstrably, within objective cause-and-effect phenomena?

Rationalising the absurd

To put it another way, for clarity: we perceive causality with our minds – so, in a way, it can be regarded as a psychic event. Experiment proves that causality always obtains in 'outer', objective events so we know that it, too, has an objective existence. But equally, we perceive acausal connections (meaningful coincidences) with our minds, so we know that acausality is a mental – or psychic – phenomenon. Could it also be that it actually happens in the outer world, and so has an objective existence of its own?

In short, might it not be that acausality is a cardinal structural principle of connection that lies at the very foundation of outer reality, a fourth to join the great triad of space, time and causality?

The implications of the idea are almost too difficult to imagine – in part, as Jung was the first to appreciate, because to pursue the possibilities further involves the extraordinary task of setting the psyche to investigate the deeper reaches of itself. But this is, of course, the central purpose of depth psychology. And the rewards for attempting such a piece of research could be immense – Jung's idea of synchronicity does, at the very least, indicate vast frontiers, philosophical as well as psychological, that await exploration.

Jung made his pioneering steps untroubled by his awareness that he would have to travel along some paths in the 'dark and dubious' areas that orthodox science is inclined to dismiss as superstition – mankind's ancient and still thriving traditions of divination, magic and the paranormal. We may still hope that a time will come when fear, prejudice and mental laziness will no longer prevent other people from setting out to determine whether Jung's idea of synchronicity may indeed lead to new ways of perceiving the nature of mind, the nature of matter – and the nature of Nature itself.

The case of the Cottingley fairies

All of us, when we were children, believed in fairies. Here, JOE COOPER tells the extraordinary story of two little girls who not only believed in fairies, but made friends with them — and even captured them on film

IN THE WEEK BEFORE the end of the First World War, 11-year-old Frances Griffiths sent a letter to a friend in South Africa, where she had lived most of her life. Dated 9 November 1918, it ran:

Dear Joe [Johanna],

I hope you are quite well. I wrote a letter before, only I lost it or it got mislaid. Do you play with Elsie and Nora Biddles? I am learning French, Geometry, Cookery and Algebra at school now. Dad came home from France the other week after being there ten months, and we all think the war will be over in a few days. We are going to get our flags to hang upstairs in our bedroom. I am sending two photos, both of me, one of me in a bathing costume in our back yard, Uncle Arthur took that, while the other is me with some fairies up the beck, Elsie took that one. Rosebud is as

Above: a sharpened version of the first photograph (right), which shows Frances Griffiths behind a group of dancing fairies. Photographic experts examined the negative and the print but could find no trace of trickery

fat as ever and I have made her some new clothes. How are Teddy and dolly?

An ordinary and matter-of-fact letter from a schoolgirl to her friend, one might say, apart from the rather startling reference to fairies. But, as both Frances and her cousin Elsie Wright have since pointed out (they are now grandmothers), they were not particularly surprised by seeing fairies; they seemed a natural part of the rural countryside around the 'beck' (stream) at the bottom of the long garden in Cottingley, near Bradford, in West Yorkshire.

The photograph enclosed by Frances — the famous one, which has since been reproduced thousands of times around the world, albeit in an improved and sharpened version — showed a little girl staring firmly at a camera, since fairies were frequently to be seen, but she herself was photographed not so often! On the back of the snap was scrawled in untidy schoolgirl writing:

Elsie and I are very friendly with the beck Fairies. It is funny I never used to see them in Africa. It must be too hot for them there.

Elsie had borrowed her father's camera – a Midg quarter-plate – one Saturday afternoon in July 1917 in order to take Frances's photo and cheer her up (for her cousin had fallen in the beck and been scolded for wetting her clothes). They were away for about half an hour and Mr Wright developed the plate later in the afternoon. He was surprised to see strange white shapes coming up, imagining them to be first birds and then sandwich papers left lying around; in vain Elsie behind him in the dark-room said they were fairies.

In August it was Frances who had the camera, when she and Elsie scaled the sides of the beck and went up to the old oaks. There she took a photograph of Elsie with a gnome. The print was under-exposed and unclear, as might be expected when taken by a young lady rising 10 years old. The plate was again developed by Elsie's father, Arthur, who suspected that the girls had been playing tricks and refused to lend his camera to them any more.

Parents turn sleuth

Both Arthur and his wife, Polly, searched the girls' bedroom and waste-paper basket for any scraps of pictures or cut-outs, and also went down to the beck in search of evidence of fakery. They found nothing, and the girls stuck to their story – that they had seen fairies and photographed them. Prints of the pictures were circulated among friends and neighbours, but then interest in the odd affair gradually petered out.

The matter first became public in the summer of 1919 when Polly Wright went to a meeting at the Theosophical Society in Bradford. She was interested in the occult, having had some experiences of astral projection and memories of past lives herself. The lecture that night was on 'fairy life', and Polly mentioned to the person sitting next to her that fairy prints had been taken by her daughter and niece. The result of this conversation was that two 'rough prints' (as they were later called) came to the notice of Theosophists at the Harrogate conference in the autumn, and thence to a leading Theosophist, Edward Gardner, by early 1920.

Mr Gardner was a precise, particular man. Even a look at his photograph conveys this precision, which is also suggested by the neat copies he kept of his letters. Gardner's immediate impulse after seeing the fairy pictures was to clarify the prints and, in a letter to a photographic expert, Fred Barlow, he describes the instructions he gave to his assistants:

Then I told them to make new negatives (from the positives of the originals) and do the very best with them

Above: Sir Arthur Conan Doyle, who used sharpened prints of the first two Cottingley photographs to illustrate his article on fairies, which was published in the Christmas 1920 issue of the *Strand Magazine*

Above: Elsie Wright and her cousin Frances (above right). The girls were close companions and spent hours playing together near the beck where the fairy photographs were taken

Below: Polly Wright, Elsie's mother, began to take the photographs seriously after she had attended a Theosophical Society lecture on 'fairy life'

short of altering anything mechanically. The result was that they turned out two first class negatives which . . . are the same in every respect as the originals except that they are sharp cut and clear and far finer for printing purposes . . .

It seems incredible to us today that he could be so naïve, not anticipating the inevitable questions from critics as to shutter speed, figure definition, the suspicious resemblance of the fairies' clothes and hairstyles to the latest fashions . . . But Gardner only wanted the clearest pictures – as a Theosophist he had been studying fairy lore for years and had heard many accounts of fairy sightings, so the possible reactions of sceptics never entered his head.

By a striking coincidence, Sir Arthur Conan Doyle (creator of Sherlock Holmes and fanatical Spiritualist) had been commissioned by the *Strand Magazine* to write an article on fairies for their Christmas issue, to be published at the end of November 1920. He was preparing this in June when he heard of the two fairy prints in circulation and eventually made contact with Gardner and borrowed copies.

From the beginning, contrary to the impression the public later gained of him, Conan Doyle was on his guard. He showed the prints to Sir Oliver Lodge, a pioneer psychical researcher, who thought them fakes – perhaps involving a troupe of dancers masquerading as fairies. One fairy authority told him that the hairstyles of the sprites were too 'Parisienne' for his liking. Lodge also passed them on to a clairvoyant for psychometric impressions – Gardner's photoprinter, Mr Snelling (who had prepared the second batch of prints from the originals) was described accurately.

What seems rather mysterious to us today is that no one was over-anxious to examine the original photographs, but seemed content to analyse prints. Snelling (of whom it had been said 'What Snelling doesn't know about faked photography isn't worth knowing') said in his first report to Gardner on the

Above: a sharpened print of 'Elsie and the gnome', the second fairy photograph, which was taken by Frances in August 1917. The original was examined by experts in the same way as the first – again no evidence of fakery could be found

Below: Arthur Wright, Elsie's father, whose camera – a Midg quarter-plate – was used to take the photographs

'rough' print that he could detect movement in all the fairy figures. Kodak, by contrast, stated that an experienced photographer may have been involved – which suggests that the prints that they had been examining may have been sharpened ones.

A possible explanation is that Conan Doyle and Gardner may have wished to avoid any mention of improving the originals at that stage; perhaps they did not consider the matter important. What was vital to them was the propagation of Theosophical and Spiritualist doctrines. As far as they were concerned, clear prints showing recognisable fairies and a gnome would provide the long-sought firm evidence for 'dwellers at the border' (as Conan Doyle was later to term nature spirits).

Conan Doyle despatched his 'Watson' – in this real-life case, Gardner – to Cottingley in July. Gardner reported that the whole Wright family seemed honest and totally respectable. Conan Doyle and Gardner decided that if further fairy photographs were taken then the matter would be put firmly beyond question. Gardner journeyed north in August with cameras and 20 photographic

plates to leave with Elsie and Frances hoping to persuade them to take more photographs. Only in this way, he felt, could it be proved that the fairies were genuine.

Meanwhile, the *Strand* article was completed, featuring the two sharpened prints, and Conan Doyle sailed for Australia and a lecture tour to spread the gospel of Spiritualism. He left his colleagues to face the public reactions to the fairy business.

Newspaper sensation

That issue of the *Strand* sold out within days of publication at the end of November. Reaction was vigorous – especially from critics. The leading voice among them was that of one Major Hall-Edwards, a radium expert. He declared:

> On the evidence I have no hesitation in saying that these photographs could have been 'faked'. I criticise the attitude of those who declared there is something supernatural in the circumstances attending to the taking of these pictures because, as a medical man, I believe that the inculcation of such absurd ideas into the minds of children will result in later life in manifestations and nervous disorder and mental disturbances . . .

Newspaper comments were varied. On 5 January 1921 *Truth* declared: 'For the true explanation of these fairy photographs what is wanted is not a knowledge of occult phenomena but a knowledge of children.' On the other hand the *South Wales Argus* of 27 November 1920 took a more whimsical and tolerant view: 'The day we kill our Santa Claus with our statistics we shall have plunged a glorious world into deepest darkness'. The Day's Thought underneath was a Welsh proverb: ''Tis true as the fairy tales told in books.' *City News*, on 29 January, said straightforwardly: 'It seems at this point that we must either believe in the almost incredible mystery of the fairy or in the almost incredible wonders of faked photographs.'

The *Westminster Gazette* broke the aliases used by Conan Doyle to protect Frances and Elsie – and a reporter went north. However, nothing sensational, or even new, was added to the story by his investigation. He found out that Elsie had borrowed her father's camera to take the first picture, and that Frances had taken a picture of Elsie and a gnome. In fact there was nothing he could add to the facts listed by Conan Doyle in his article 'Fairies photographed – an epoch-making event'. The reporter considered Polly and Arthur Wright to be honest enough folk – and he returned a verdict of 'unexplained' to his paper in London.

The case might well have faded away with the coming of spring in 1921, had not the unexpected happened: Elsie and Frances took three more fairy photographs.

The reappearance of the fairies

The Cottingley 'fairy' pictures provoked heated argument. To Sir Arthur Conan Doyle they were the long-awaited proof of the existence of spirits – but to many people they were just clever fakes.

IN THE SCHOOL HOLIDAYS of August 1920, Frances Griffiths was asked to come by train to Cottingley from Scarborough, where she had gone to live with her mother and father after the First World War. Aunt Polly had written to say that Edward Gardner would be travelling up from London, with new cameras, so that the cousins might have further opportunities of taking fairy photographs to add to the two they took in 1917.

Frances was a month away from her 14th birthday and had won a scholarship to go to grammar school, being both industrious and intelligent. Elsie, by contrast, had thankfully left school at the age of 13.

Edward Gardner came from London to Bradford by train and took the tram out to Cottingley Bar, three miles (5 kilometres) away. He had brought with him two cameras and two dozen secretly marked photographic plates. He described the briefing of the girls thus in his book *Fairies: a book of real fairies* published in 1945:

> I went off, too, to Cottingley again, taking the two cameras and plates from London, and met the family and explained to the two girls the simple working of the cameras, giving one each to keep. The cameras were loaded, and my final advice was that they need go up to the glen only on fine days as they had been accustomed to do before and tice the fairies, as they called their way of attracting them, and see what they could get. I suggested only the most obvious and easy precautions about lighting and distance, for I knew it was essential they should feel free and unhampered and have no burden of responsibility. If nothing came of it all, I told them, they were not to mind a bit.

Only two more fairies

One might imagine the scene in the parlour of the Wright household. Beautiful Polly, listening intently, gangly 19-year-old Elsie with her auburn gold hair and gentle blue eyes, and sharp Frances, her energies suppressed for the occasion. ('Pity anyone with corns who is around when Frances gets excited,' Polly had written wryly on one occasion.) And solemn Edward Gardner, bearded and perhaps sporting a bow tie as usual, eager to engender some sort of scientific atmosphere but, in his heart, really not hoping for very much, in spite of the new cameras and carefully marked plates. So he returned to London, hoping for fine weather at least.

Alas, it rained for two weeks. They had little opportunity of adding anything to fairy history, and the first record of anything happening is in a letter to Gardner from

Left: a fairy offering flowers to Elsie, 1920. Elsie Wright said that the flowers were tiny harebells, and that the colours of the fairy's dress were pastel shades of mauve and yellow. This particular Cottingley photograph prompted widespread criticism: the fairy has a suspiciously contemporary appearance, with its bobbed hair and fashionable dress

Polly, which is truly astounding in its modesty. She wrote about the events of Thursday, 19 August 1920:

> The morning was dull and misty so they did not take any photos until after dinner when the mist had cleared away and it was sunny. I went to my sister's for tea and left them to it. When I got back they had only managed two with fairies, I was disappointed.

and about those of two days after:

> They went up again on Saturday afternoon and took several photos but there was only one with anything on and it's a queer one, we can't make it out. Elsie put the plates in this time and Arthur developed them next day.

and what must rank as one of the most charming postscripts ever: 'P.S. She did not take one flying after all.'

So the plates were returned to London. Elsie remembers the care with which they were packed in cotton wool by her father, who was puzzled – about the whole affair. He never understood it until the end of his days (he died in 1926) and Conan Doyle went down in his estimation. Before the great man had shown an interest in fairies, Arthur held him in high regard; afterwards he found it hard to believe that so intelligent a man could be bamboozled 'by our Elsie, and her at the bottom of the class!' But whereas Arthur could not bring himself to believe in fairies, Polly, as the tone of her letter suggests, supported her daughter and acknowledged the existence of nature spirits.

Gardner was elated to receive the secretly marked plates which bore such intriguing fairy photographs and telegrams were sent off to Conan Doyle who was on his Australian lecture tour, currently in Melbourne. Conan Doyle wrote back:

> My heart was gladdened when out here in far Australia I had your note and the

Above: Frances and the leaping fairy, taken by Elsie from a distance of about 3 feet (1 metre). The fairy was said to be leaping, not flying, as it appears to be. It bounded up in the air four times before Elsie took the picture. The fifth leap was so vigorous that Frances thought it was jumping at her face and flung her head back; the movement can be seen in the print

three wonderful pictures which are confirmatory of our published results. When our fairies are admitted other psychic phenomena will find a more ready acceptance . . . we have had continued messages at seances for some time that a visible sign was coming through . . .

Both Conan Doyle and Edward Gardner were primarily interested in spreading their own ideas of the infinite to what they considered to be a far from receptive public. Conan Doyle saw the Cottingley fairies incident as (perhaps literally) a gift from the gods, paving the way for more profound truths that may gradually become acceptable to a materialistic world. He used the last three photographs to illustrate a second article in the *Strand Magazine* in 1921. It described other accounts of alleged fairy sightings and served as the foundation for his later book entitled *The coming of the fairies*, published in 1922.

Reactions to the new fairy photographs were, as before, varied. The most common criticism was that the fairies looked suspiciously like the traditional fairies of nursery tales and that they had very fashionable hairstyles. It was also pointed out that the pictures were particularly sharply-defined, as if some improvement had been made by an expert photographer.

However, some public figures were sympathetic – sometimes embarrassingly so. Margaret McMillan, the educational and social reformer (who, among other reforms,

Above: the 'fairy bower' long believed by some fairylorists to exist, but, as Conan Doyle exclaimed, 'Never before, or other where [*sic*], has a fairy's bower been photographed!' The cocoon-like structure is said to be used by fairies to bathe in after long spells of dull and misty weather

Below: Cottingley as it was in the 1920s

brought the benefits of public baths to the slum children of Bradford), waxed fulsome about the Cottingley incidents: 'How wonderful that to these dear children such a wonderful gift has been vouchsafed.'

Another eminent personality of the day, the novelist Henry de Vere Stacpoole, decided to take the fairy photographs – and the girls – at face value. He accepted intuitively that both girls and pictures were genuine. In a letter to Gardner he said:

Look at Alice's face. Look at Iris's face. There is an extraordinary thing called TRUTH which has 10 million faces and forms – it is God's currency and the cleverest coiner or forger can't imitate it . . .

(The aliases 'Alice' and 'Iris' first used by Conan Doyle to protect the anonymity of the girls were deliberately preserved by Stacpoole.)

'Fed up with fairies!'

The fifth, and last, fairy photograph is often believed to be the most striking. Nobody has ever been able to give a satisfactory explanation as to what seems to be happening in the picture. However, Conan Doyle, in his *The coming of the fairies* advances a detailed, if somewhat over-elaborate, view of the pictured proceedings:

Seated on the upper left hand edge with wing well displayed is an undraped fairy apparently considering whether it is time to get up. An earlier riser of more mature age is seen on the right possessing abundant hair and wonderful wings. Her slightly denser body can be glimpsed within her fairy dress.

This piece of whimsy from the creator of that most unsentimental and coldly logical character in English fiction – Sherlock Holmes – provided the 'Conan Doyle's going soft' school with formidable ammunition. It is perhaps unfortunate that his ardent interest in Spiritualism should coincide with his

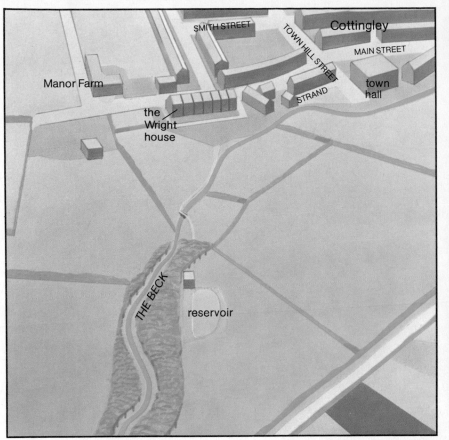

later years, especially in an age when anyone in his or her sixties was very much considered 'past their best'. His championship of the Cottingley fairies did little to dispel the growing image of him as a gullible old man. However, he was by no means the only believer in elemental spirits.

As can be seen from a map of Cottingley, it is virtually on the outskirts of populous Bradford, and is not, as many imagine, an isolated village. There is a reservoir and an old water bridge over the 'beck' – key markers for the fairy photographs. Traditionally nature spirits inhabit wooded and watery places and there are many stories of nature spirits being observed in such secluded spots. Also, the oak, ash and thorn are traditionally associated with fairies and these varieties of tree are found around the beck.

In August 1921, a last expedition was made to Cottingley – this time the clairvoyant, Geoffrey Hodson, was brought along to verify any fairy sightings. (The feeling being that if anyone, apart from the girls, could see the fairies, Hodson could.) Alas, the fairies refused to be photographed – although they were seen both by Hodson and by Elsie.

But by then both Elsie and Frances were tired of the whole fairy business. Many years later, Elsie looked at a photograph of herself and Frances taken with Hodson and said: 'Look at that – fed up with fairies!' Both Elsie and Frances have since agreed that they humoured Hodson to a sometimes ludicrous extent. This naïve admission played right into the hands of their critics. Quite apart

from 'playing Mr Hodson along' there were still the allegations of faking the whole fairy business in the first place and when more fairy photographs were not forthcoming, the 'Cottingley incident' seemed all set to be relegated to the dusty gallery of 'famous fakes'. Yet the episode is not closed. . . .

Above left: a map of the Cottingley area, showing the 'beck' where Elsie and Frances claimed to have photographed the fairies

Above: Geoffrey Hodson, a clairvoyant recommended by Sir Arthur Conan Doyle, pictured here with Elsie, aged 20, and Frances, 14, in 1921. He had personal experience of fairies and gnomes and was to publish his *Fairies at work and play* in 1922

Left: Bernard Partridge's famous caricature of the aging Conan Doyle. Though still chained by public opinion to his great fictional character Sherlock Holmes, he is seen with his head in the clouds of Spiritualism

The Cottingley fairies revisited

Ever since two young girls took 'fairy photographs' in the 1920s controversy has raged over their authenticity.

THE FIRST PHOTOGRAPH of fairies taken by Elsie Wright of Cottingley, near Bradford, in 1917 has threatened to become overexposed in the occult-conscious late 20th century, for the photograph of the sprites pictured in front of a pleasant-faced Frances has been reproduced so often that it is in danger of becoming a sort of visual cliché. It is especially irritating to those who find the whole fairy business distasteful, even fraudulent; they object, shrilly at times, to the strangely artificial look of the fairy dancers – although they are less vocal on the other four photographs that were subsequently taken. The believers, as always, believe, and speak of 'more things in Heaven and Earth . . .'

The position of critics on the one hand and champions on the other may be summed up thus:

The 'prosecution' points out that Elsie painted and drew well, that she had always seemed immersed in drawing fairies, had been fascinated by the art of photography and had worked at a photographer's, and seemed suspiciously evasive in the 1971 BBC-TV *Nationwide* interview. Both Elsie and her cousin Frances admit to a strong sense of humour; both admit to having deceived the medium Geoffrey Hodson during the 1921 investigation (in terms of giving overgenerous endorsements to his descriptions of teeming fairy life in and around the beck). No third party was ever present when the five photographs were taken. The girls spent hours together playing down at the beck, which was well away from the house and concealed, by 40-foot (12-metre) banks, from public view. They shared a fair-sized attic bedroom in which they could have hatched their plots. In 1978 the 'Amazing Randi' (a professional American stage illusionist and self-appointed debunker of all paranormal phenomena) and a team from *New Scientist* subjected the photographs to 'enhancement' – a process used to bring out greater detail from Moon photographs – and thought they could see strings attached to some figures. Randi also pointed out that the figures in the first photograph bore a resemblance to those in an illustration in *Princess Mary's gift book*, published in 1914.

The 'defence' asserts that Elsie's job at the photographer's lasted only six months and amounted to running errands and cleaning up prints. She drew fairies because she saw

Above: the young Elsie Wright's watercolour *Fairies flying over a cottage*. She often painted fairies, because, she said, she often saw them

Left: an illustration from *Princess Mary's gift book*, which was very popular in 1914. These fairies bear some resemblance to those allegedly seen and photographed at Cottingley

Most people do not believe in fairies and therefore, to them, any alleged fairy photographs must be fakes. To sceptics there is no question about it: the Cottingley fairies were cut out of a children's book and superimposed, very cleverly (for no one has conclusively proved that they were faked), on photographs of the cousins, Elsie and Frances.

There was no shortage of material had they wanted to search for fairy 'models'. Fairies were common enough in children's books around the turn of the century. Most girls of their age, living at that time, could have described a fairy, for most illustrations reflected a similar, traditional fairy image.

In fact, Elsie and Frances's fairies were, if anything, slightly more fashion-conscious than, say, those pictured in the popular *Princess Mary's gift book* of 1914. The Cottingley fairies had up-to-the-minute bobbed hair and beaded Charleston dresses (although Elsie's gnome remained traditionally grotesque).

When psychical researcher E.L. Gardner visited Cottingley in the 1920s

Several critics pointed out that the Cottingley fairies looked suspiciously similar to those featured in the advertisement for Price's night lights (above right). One sceptic, William Marriott, produced this deliberate fake (above left) by superimposing the 'night light' fairies on a picture of Sir Arthur Conan Doyle

Some fairies of the era: Left: fairies dancing, by E. Gertrude Thomson from William Allingham's *The fairies* (1886)

Above: a ring of fairies from Florence Harrison's *In the fairy ring* (1910)

Above right: a girl with fairies, from *Princess Mary's gift book* (1914)

he claimed mediumistic powers for both girls, but especially for Frances. He believed that the elemental spirits – fairies – used loosely-knit ectoplasm emanating from the girls with which to form visible bodies, visible, that is, only to the girls and the eye of the camera. The exact form they took was, he hazarded, 'chosen' by the subconscious minds of the girls, hence the strange mixture of traditional and contemporary. But, for whatever reason, both girls stopped seeing fairies after 1921.

them often and, anyway, her drawings were no better than might be expected from a fairly talented 16-year-old. As for the *Gift book* illustrations – fairies dancing around are bound to resemble each other and the ones in the Christmas 1914 publication lack wings. The string in the report in *New Scientist* of 3 August 1978 may be printing streaks, and even real figures would not stay absolutely motionless in the breeze that usually blew gently down the beck; and where might they be hung from? And what variety of invisible 'string' was used at the time? By the time Hodson came they were bored and nodded confirmation for the sake of peace and quiet. Elsie prevaricated because she wanted the matter to be forgotten. They did not have the motivation, materials, time, privacy, or expertise to fake the photographs. And, most significantly, they have always maintained they saw fairies and photographed them.

Newspapers, magazines and television companies have become increasingly interested in Elsie and Frances since Peter Chambers of the *Daily Express* discovered where Elsie lived in 1966. He quotes Elsie as saying that the fairies might have been 'figments of

Below: *Fairies by a stream*, a watercolour by Elsie Wright. She and her cousin were obsessed with fairies when they were young and this obsession is used by both the 'defence' and the 'prosecution' to explain the photographs. The sceptics use it to explain the motivation behind the 'fakes' and the believers claim that the obsession arose quite naturally because the girls saw fairies all the time

my imagination'. She may have made this rather bald statement simply to rid herself of unwelcome publicity. On the other hand she may have implied that she had successfully photographed these 'figments' of her 'imagination'. Significantly, in the years since the Cottingley fairies were photographed, research into 'thoughtography' (notably Dr Jule Eisenbud's work with Ted Serios in the United States) and experiments in Japan have indicated that thoughtforms may indeed be photographed.

Elsie and Frances interrogated

For five years Elsie managed to avoid publicity; then, in 1971, BBC-TV's *Nationwide* programme took up the case. For 10 days she was interrogated, taken back to Cottingley and subjected to this sort of thing:

(The interviewer points out that, since the original fairy investigator, E. L. Gardner, died the year before, Elsie might wish to be more explicit.)
Elsie: I didn't want to upset Mr Gardner . . . I don't mind talking now . . .
(It is then suggested that Elsie's father had a hand in matters.)
Elsie: I would swear on the Bible father didn't know what was going on.
Interviewer: Could you equally swear on the Bible you didn't play any tricks?
Elsie (after a pause): I took the photographs . . . I took two of them . . . no, three . . . Frances took two . . .
Interviewer: Are they trick photographs? Could you swear on the Bible about that?
Elsie (after a pause): I'd rather leave that open if you don't mind . . . but my father had nothing to do with it I can promise you that . . .
Interviewer: Have you had your fun with the world for 50 years? Have you been kidding us for 10 days?
(Elsie laughs.)
Elsie (gently): I think we'll close on that if you don't mind.

More objective was Austin Mitchell's interview for Yorkshire Television in September 1976. On the spot where the photographs had allegedly been taken, the following dialogue took place:
Mitchell: A rational person doesn't see fairies. If people say they see fairies, then one's bound to be critical.
Frances: Yes.
Mitchell: Now, if you say you saw them, at the time the photograph was taken, that means that if there's a confidence trick, then you're both part of it.
Frances: Yes – that's fair enough – yes.
Mitchell: So are you?
Frances: No.
Elsie: No.
Frances: Of course not.
Mitchell: Did you, in any way, fabricate those photographs?
Frances: Of course not. You tell us how she could do it – remember she was 16 and I was

10. Now then, as a child of 10, can you go through life and keep a secret?

The Yorkshire Television team, however, believed the 'cardboard cutout' theory. Austin Mitchell duly appeared on the screen, personable as ever, with a row of fairy figures before him set against a background of greenery. He flicked them around a little (perhaps to reassure viewers that elementals had not invaded the prosaic surroundings of Kirkstall Road, Leeds).

'Simple cardboard cutouts,' he commented on the live magazine programme. 'Done by our photographic department and mounted on wire frames. They discovered that you really need wire to make them stand up – paper figures droop, of course. That's how it could have been done.'

But quite apart from the pronouncements of critics and champions, tapes, letters and newspaper cuttings are now available for anyone who would delve deeper into the fairy photographs. Understandably, Elsie and Frances would rather people kept away and respected their privacy after the passage of so many years.

The critics – Lewis of *Nationwide*, Austin Mitchell of Yorkshire TV, Randi, and Stewart Sanderson and Katherine Briggs of the Folklore Society – all these are fair-minded individuals interested in balancing probability on the available evidence. This extremely delicate balance did seem to have shifted in favour of the ladies' honesty during

Above: a rare 'cup and ring' stone, found in Cottingley Glen, close to the beck. Such strangely marked stones are traditionally associated with supernatural activities and have often been linked with fairy sightings

the 1970s but, obviously, many points could still be elucidated by further research.

Austin Mitchell said 'a rational person doesn't see fairies', and there are some sociologists who would say that rationality might be socially constructed. One's 'rationality' mostly depends on one's personal experiences and one's reading. There are, believe it or not, hundreds of instances of people claiming to have seen fairies. A perusal of Conan Doyle's book *The coming of the fairies*, or *Visions or beliefs* by Lady Gregory and the poet W. B. Yeats, should prove that more than a handful of such claims have been made.

The author has now met seven people who claim to have seen nature spirits. One of them, an ex-wrestler of powerful build – an unlikely figure to consort with sprites – is adamant in his assertions. It is interesting to note how many are prepared to listen to him with an unusual degree of tolerance.

It is usually possible to demolish individual accounts; taken collectively, however, some patterns begin to emerge. F. W. Holiday in his book *The dragon and the disc* likens the appearance of the Cottingley gnome to that of Icelandic Bronze Age figures, and William Riley, the Yorkshire author, puts the five fairy pictures into perhaps the most relevant context: 'I have many times come across several people who have seen pixies at certain favoured spots in Upper Airedale and Wharfedale.'

Defying the law of gravity

The power to overcome the force of gravity may be the product of long training, or may occur spontaneously, amazing levitator and onlookers alike. LYNN PICKNETT surveys some famous cases of this extraordinary talent

THREE NOTABLE MEMBERS of London society witnessed, on 16 December 1868, an incident so extraordinary that it is still the focus of controversy. Viscount Adare, the Master of Lindsay and Captain Wynne saw the famous medium Daniel Dunglas Home rise into the air and float out of one window in a large house in fashionable London and then float in at another – over 80 feet (24 metres) from the ground it is claimed. D. D. Home became known primarily for his levitations, of himself and of objects – on one occasion a grand piano – but he was not alone in having this 'impossible' ability to defy the law of gravity.

St Joseph of Copertino (1603–1663) flew into the air every time he was emotionally excited. Being of an excitable nature, he often made levitations, and they were well witnessed. A simple peasant – some say he was actually feeble-minded – this boy from Apulia, Italy, spent his youth trying to achieve religious ecstasy by such means as self-flagellation, starvation and wearing hair-shirts. He became a Franciscan at the age of 22, and then his religious fervour 'took off' quite literally.

St Joseph and his 'giddiness'

Joseph became something of an embarrassment to his superiors. During Mass one Sunday he rose into the air and flew onto the altar in the midst of the candles; he was quite badly burned as a result.

For 35 years Joseph was excluded from all public services because of his disconcerting habits, but still tales of his levitations spread. While walking with a Benedictine monk in the monastery gardens he suddenly flew up into an olive tree. Unfortunately he couldn't fly back down, so his fellow-monks had to fetch a ladder.

A surgeon, at least two cardinals and one Pope (Urban VIII), among many others, witnessed Joseph's extraordinary spells of weightlessness – which he called 'my giddinesses'. He spent his entire life in a state of prayer, and the Church concluded the levitations must be the work of God.

Another levitating saint was St Teresa of Avila, who died in 1582. This remarkable mystic experienced the same feelings as many people feel during the common 'flying dreams'. She described how she felt about her levitations:

It seemed to me, when I tried to make some resistance, as if a great force

Above: D. D. Home, who ascribed his levitations to the work of spirits

Above right: Home floats into the air with no visible means of support

Below: St Joseph of Copertino owed his canonisation to his ability to levitate

beneath my feet lifted me up. . . . I confess that it threw me into great fear, very great indeed at first; for in seeing one's body thus lifted up from the earth, though the spirit draws it upwards after itself (and that with great sweetness, if unresisted) the senses are not lost; at least I was so much myself as able to see that I was being lifted up. After the rapture was over, I have to say my body seemed frequently to be buoyant, as if all weight had departed from it, so much so that now and then I scarce knew my feet touched the ground.

So insistent were her levitations that she begged the sisters to hold her down when she felt an 'attack' coming on, but often there was no time for preventive measures – she simply rose off the floor until the weightlessness passed.

Most levitators are believers in one particular system, be it Christianity, Hindu mysticism, ancient Egyptian mysteries or Spiritualism. It was to this last category that D. D. Home belonged.

Born in Scotland and brought up in America, Home was a puny, artistic child. At the age of 13 he had a vision of a friend, Edwin. Home announced to his aunt's family

that it must mean that Edwin had been dead for three days. This was proved to be true. Home's career as a medium had begun – but it was not until he was 19 that he was to defy the law of gravity.

Ward Cheney, a prosperous silk-manufacturer, held a seance at his home in Connecticut in August 1852. D. D. Home was there to provide the usual 'spiritualist' manifestations – table-turning, rappings, floating trumpets and mysterious lights.

Home was quite capable of keeping the guests entertained in this fashion but something happened, completely unannounced, that made his name overnight. He floated up into the air until his head was touching the ceiling. Among the guests was the sceptical reporter, F. L. Burr, editor of the *Hartford Times*. He wrote of this bizarre and unexpected incident:

Suddenly, without any expectation on the part of the company, Home was taken up into the air. I had hold of his hand at the time and I felt his feet – they were lifted a foot [30 centimetres] from the floor. He palpitated from head to foot with the contending emotions of joy and fear which choked his utterances. Again and again he was taken from the floor, and the third time he was carried to the ceiling of the apartment, with which his hands and feet came into gentle contact.

Home's career advanced rapidly; he was lionised in seance parlour and royal court alike. He came back to Europe to inspire adoration and scepticism (Robert Browning's

Top: Colin Evans apparently drifting aloft at the Conway Hall, London, in the 1930s

Above: St Teresa of Avila was subject to 'attacks' of levitation

Left: away from all artificial aids, this couple defeats the force of gravity on a South African beach in 1962

satirical poem 'Mr Sludge' was based on his own biased view of the medium). Wherever he went there were bizarre phenomena – winds howled in still rooms, apports of fresh flowers fell from the ceiling, doors opened and shut, fireballs zigzagged around the room – and Home levitated.

The famous occasion already mentioned when he floated out of one window and in through another, is still the subject of heated debate, particularly since the incident was documented by respectable witnesses. One of them, the Master of Lindsay (later the Earl of Crawford) wrote:

I was sitting with Mr Home and Lord Adare and a cousin of his [Captain Wynne]. During the sitting Mr Home went into a trance and in that state was carried out of the window in the room next to where we were, and was brought in at our window. The distance between the windows was about seven feet six inches [2.3 metres], and there was not the slightest foothold between them, nor was there more than a 12-inch [30-centimetre] projection to each window, which served as a ledge to put flowers on. We heard the window in the next room lift up, and almost immediately after we saw Home floating in the air outside our window. The moon was shining full into the room; my back was to the light, and I saw the shadow on the wall of the windowsill, and Home's feet about six inches [15 centimetres] above it. He remained in this position for a few seconds, then raised the window and glided into the room feet foremost and sat down.

Sceptics such as Frank Podmore or, more recently, John Sladek, have tried to disprove

Top: the classic stage levitation. The girl, Marva Ganzel, is first hypnotised into a cataleptic trance while balanced on two swords. When one is taken away, she somehow remains suspended in mid-air

Above: Frank Podmore, who suggested that D. D. Home's most famous levitation was merely an hallucination

Right: accounts of levitation and other manifestations of the seance room did not impress *Punch*, which in 1863 published this lampoon, showing that some surprises, at least, could be administered by all too explicable means

this levitation, although neither of them was among the witnesses. Sladek attempts to discredit the three who were present by comparing the details of their stories – such as how high the balconies were from the street, or indeed, whether there were any balconies at all.

Podmore, on the other hand, is more subtle in his scepticism. He mentions the fact that a few days before the levitation, and in front of the same witnesses, Home had opened the window and stood on the ledge outside. He had pointedly drawn their attention to himself standing on the narrow ledge some considerable distance from the ground. Podmore remarked drily 'the medium had thus, as it were, furnished a rough sketch of the picture which he aimed at producing.' On another occasion Home suddenly announced 'I'm rising, I'm rising', before proceeding to levitate in front of several witnesses.

Podmore implied that Home's levitations were nothing more than hallucinations produced by his hypnotic suggestion, rather in the same manner that the Indian rope trick is said to be a mass hallucination, the secret being in the magician's patter.

But even in the face of extreme hostility, Home remained a successful levitator for over 40 years. Among his witnesses were Emperor Napoleon III, John Ruskin and Bulwer Lytton – and many hundreds more, not all of whom were as inconsistent in their testimonies as Adare, Wynne and Lindsay. Moreover during that long span of time and mostly in broad daylight, Home was never proved to be a fraud. And despite Podmore's accusations Home never went out of his way to build up an atmosphere heavy with suggestibility. In fact, he was one of the few

Ridicule has long been poured on the notion that people can free themselves from the force of gravity: this cartoon (left), entitled 'The Day's Folly', was published by Sergent in 1783. But Alexandra David-Neel (below) came back from 14 years in Tibet with no doubt that adepts could achieve weightlessness

mediums who actively eschewed 'atmosphere' – he preferred a normal or bright light to darkness and encouraged the sitters to chat normally rather than 'hold hands and concentrate'.

Although in his mature years Home could levitate at will, he apparently also levitated without being aware of it. On one occasion, when his host drew his attention to the fact that he was hovering above the cushions of his armchair, Home seemed most surprised.

Stage illusionists frequently pride themselves on their *pièce de résistance*; putting their assistant into a 'trance', balancing her on the points of two swords – then removing the swords so that she hangs in the air without apparent support. Sometimes she is 'hypnotised' and seen to rise further into the air – still without visible means of support. One of two things must be happening: either she does not rise into the air at all (that is, we

all suffer a mass hallucination) or she rises aided by machinery invisible to us.

Of course, Home and other spiritualists would also attribute their feats of apportation or levitation to 'machinery invisible to us' – but in their case the machinery would be the agency of spirits. To the end of his life, Home maintained that he could only fly through the air because he was lifted up by the spirits, who thus demonstrated their existence. But he described a typical levitation as follows:

> I feel no hands supporting me, and, since the first time, I have never felt fear; though, should I have fallen from the ceiling of some rooms in which I have been raised, I could not have escaped serious injury. I am generally lifted up perpendicularly; my arms frequently become rigid, and are drawn above my head, as if I were grasping the unseen power which slowly raises me from the floor.

The gravity enigma

And yet we do not refer in this spiritualistic way to the 'unseen power' that keeps us *on* the floor. Every schoolboy knows about Newton and his discovery of the law of gravity. But psychical research points to the relative ease with which certain sensitives can turn this law on its head.

In her book *Mystère et magique en Tibet* (1931), Madame Alexandra David-Neel, the French explorer who spent 14 years in and around Tibet, told how she came upon a naked man, weighed down with heavy chains. His companion explained to her that his mystical training had made his body so light that, unless he wore iron chains, he would float away.

It would seem that gravity does not necessarily have the hold on us we have been taught it has. Sir William Crookes, the renowned scientist and psychical researcher, had this to say about D. D. Home:

> The phenomena I am prepared to attest are so extraordinary, and so directly oppose the most firmly-rooted articles of scientific belief – amongst others, the ubiquity and invariable action of the force of gravitation – that, even now, on recalling the details of what I have witnessed, there is an antagonism in my mind between *reason*, which pronounces it to be scientifically impossible, and the consciousness that my senses, both of touch and sight, are not lying witnesses.

So we conclude that in some *special* cases – such as saints or particularly gifted mediums – levitation exists. But there is a growing body of thought that puts forward the idea that anyone can do it, providing he or she has the right training – students of transcendental meditation claim to do it all the time.

The art of levitation

It is claimed that many ancient peoples knew the secrets of levitation. But it is not, apparently, a lost art: some people today claim to be able to attain weightlessness by an effort of will

A UNIQUE SERIES of photographs appeared in the magazine *Illustrated London News* on 6 June 1936. They showed the successive stages in the levitation of an Indian *yogi*, Subbayah Pullavar – thus proving that, whatever else it was, this phenomenon was not a hypnotic illusion.

A European witness of the event, P. Y. Plunkett, sets the scene:

The time was about 12.30 p.m. and the sun directly above us so that shadows played no part in the performance. . . . Standing quietly by was Subbayah Pullavar, the performer, with long hair, a drooping moustache and a wild look in his eye. He salaamed to us and stood chatting for a while. He had been practising this particular branch of yoga for nearly 20 years (as had past generations of his family). We asked permission to take photographs of the performance and he gave it willingly. . . .

Plunkett gathered together about 150 witnesses while the performer began his ritual preparations. Water was poured around the tent in which the act of levitation was to take place; leather-soled shoes were banned inside the circle, and the performer entered

Photographs taken of a levitation performance carried out by an Indian yogi, Subbayah Pullavar, before a large number of witnesses. The photographs were taken by the Englishman P. Y. Plunkett and a friend, and published in the *Illustrated London News* of 6 June 1936. The first photograph (below) shows the yogi before levitation, lying inside a tent. He is grasping a cloth-wrapped stick, which he continues to hold throughout the performance. The tent is then closed (right) for some minutes during the mysterious act of levitation itself

the tent alone. Some minutes later helpers removed the tent and there, inside the circle, was the fakir, floating on the air.

Plunkett and another witness came forward to investigate: the fakir was suspended in the air about a yard from the ground. Although he held on to a cloth-covered stick, this seemed to be for purposes of balance only – not for support. Plunkett and his friend examined the space around and under Subbayah Pullavar, and found it innocent of any strings or other 'invisible' apparatus. The yogi was in a trance and many witnesses believed that he had indisputably levitated,

As the levitation performance continues, the curtains of the tent are drawn back and the yogi appears, floating in mid-air (top). Plunkett and his friend examined the space beneath and around the yogi, but were unable to find any evidence of strings or other supporting apparatus. Although some sceptics have claimed that the yogi was, in fact, not levitating but merely in a cataleptic trance, the relaxed position of the hand on the post suggests that the body of the yogi was indeed very nearly weightless during the performance. After levitation (above right) the yogi's body was so stiff that five men could not bend his limbs

although it has been suggested that he had, in fact, merely passed into a cataleptic trance. The famous photographs were taken from various angles during the four minutes of the performance, and then the tent was re-erected around the fakir. Evidently the 'descent' was something very private, but Plunkett managed to witness it through the thin tent walls:

> After about a minute he appeared to sway and then very slowly began to descend, still in a horizontal position. He took about five minutes to move from the top of the stick to the ground, a distance of about three feet [1 metre] . . . When Subbayah was back on the ground his assistants carried him over to where we were sitting and asked if we would try to bend his limbs. Even with assistance we were unable to do so.

The yogi was rubbed and splashed with cold water for a further five minutes before he came out of his trance and regained full use of his limbs.

The swaying motion and horizontal position that Plunkett witnessed seem to be essential to true levitation. Students of transcendental meditation (TM) are taught, under the supervision of the Maharishi Mahesh Yogi at his headquarters in Switzerland, to levitate. One student described this 'impossible' achievement:

> People would rock gently, then more and more, and then start lifting off in to the air. You should really be in a lotus position to do it – you can hurt yourself landing if you've got a dangling undercarriage. To begin with it's like the Wright brothers' first flight – you come down with a bump. That's why we have to sit on foam rubber cushions. Then you learn to control it better, and it becomes totally exhilarating.

So can *anyone* induce levitation? The TM

Right: the Transcendental Meditation movement claims that this photograph shows students levitating. It is alleged that, under the supervision of tutors, the students achieve weightlessness through meditation

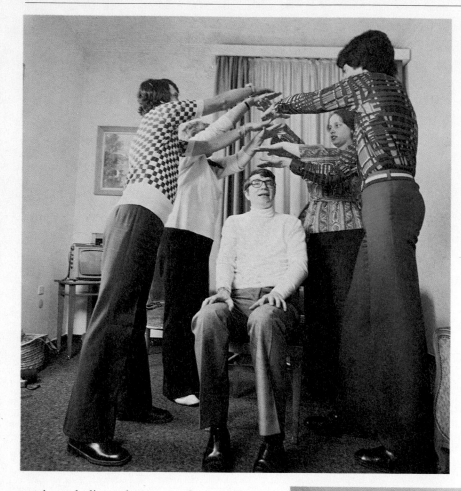

dowser's rod, intervenes to achieve the miracle of nullifying the force of gravity.

It seems that religious fervour may have something to do with the phenomenon; there are many reports of levitation by both Christian and Buddhist monks. In 1902 Aleister Crowley met his compatriot Alan Bennett, who had become a Buddhist monk, at his monastery in Burma in 1902; he, too, had become so weightless that he was 'blown about like a leaf'.

Alexandra David-Neel, the French explorer of the early 20th century, describes witnessing an extraordinary kind of long-distance running by a Tibetan lama: 'The man did not run. He seemed to lift himself from the ground proceeding by leaps. It looked as if he had been endowed with the elasticity of a ball and rebounded each time his feet touched the ground. His steps had the regularity of a pendulum.' The lama is said to have run hundreds of miles using this strange form of locomotion, keeping his eyes fixed on some far-distant goal.

The famous Russian ballet dancer Nijinsky, too, had the extraordinary ability of appearing to be almost weightless. He would jump up high and fall as lightly – and slowly – as thistledown in what was known as the 'slow vault'.

Like many inexplicable phenomena, levitation seems to be singularly useless. The distance covered is rarely more than a few

students believe they can, after a stringent mental training; the disciplines, both spiritual and physical, of the yogis seem to prepare them to defy gravity. It is fairly easy to induce a state of semi-weightlessness, as this account of a fat publican – a perfectly ordinary person – being raised in the air as a party trick shows.

The fat man sat on a chair and four people, including his small daughter, demonstrated the impossibility of lifting him with their index fingers only, placed in his armpits and the crooks of his knees. They then removed their fingers and put their hands in a pile on top of his head, taking care to interleave their hands so that no one person's two hands were touching. The four concentrated deeply for about 15 seconds; then someone gave a signal, and quickly they replaced their fingers in armpits and knees – and the fat publican floated into the air.

Sceptics might point to the intervention of non-spiritual spirits, bearing in mind the location of the event, but the phenomenon has been witnessed hundreds of times in pubs, homes, and school-yards. If it works – and one must assume it does – then how is it possible?

The sudden burst of concentration of four people with a single, 'impossible' target could, some people believe, unlock the hidden magic of the human will. Or it has been suggested that a little-known natural force, perhaps the same one that guides the

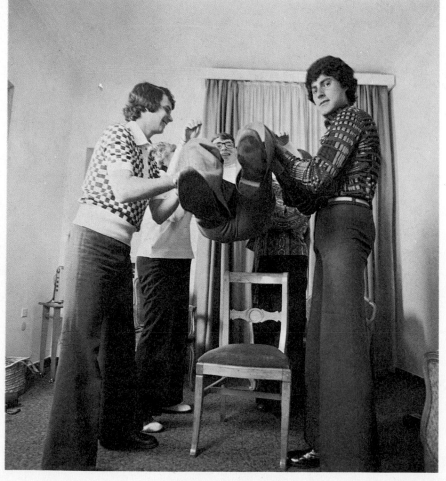

Left: an aerial view of the white horse at Uffington in Oxfordshire. The terrain on which it is carved is so hilly that its true shape can only really be appreciated from the air – a fact that has led some to speculate that the people who carved it were able to levitate and inspect their work from above

Opposite page: Uri Geller and some friends conduct a levitation session with Colin Wilson as subject. First (top) the experimenters place their hands on top of the subject's head, in such a way that no one person's two hands are touching. Then, on a command from Geller, they remove their hands from the subject's head and place their index fingers under his arms and knees. The subject immediately rises into the air (bottom)

feet or, at the most, the height of a room – useful only for dusting or decorating the home. But some people believe that the ancients could levitate quite easily, and did so to design certain enormous earthworks that can be appreciated only from the air, such as some of the white horses of the chalk downland in England and the desert patterns in Peru.

The limitations of modern levitation need not have applied to the ancients – perhaps they had developed the art to a high degree and could soar into the sky at will. Like other psychic faculties, it appears that levitation is an art, once almost lost, that is now being re-learned by determined students. Perhaps one day, modern levitators will be able to 'fly' as the ancient Druids supposedly could.

The reported 'flights' of the ancients suggest to some researchers that they were a type of out-of-the-body experience or astral travel rather than actual flesh-and-blood transportation. Certainly, many accounts of levitation or flying read like lucid dreams – and dreams of flying are very common experiences. Some dreamers wake up convinced they *can* fly; fortunately, the sights and sounds of the real world generally bring them to their senses before they can experiment.

With a few exceptions, it seems that one can levitate only after long periods of training and discipline: in this way, the body is mysteriously 'given permission' to defy the law of gravity. Perhaps there is a law of levitation with a secret formula – an 'Open, Sesame' – which the initiate uses before rising off the ground.

This theory would explain the unusual cases of spontaneous or random levitation that fascinated Charles Fort. One such case was 12-year-old Henry Jones from Shepton Mallet who, during the year 1657, was observed on several occasions to rise into the air. Once he was able to put his hands flat against the ceiling, and on another occasion he took off and sailed 30 yards (27 metres) over the garden wall. The phenomenon lasted only a year – but this was long enough for the rumour to spread that he was 'bewitched'.

Certainly levitation is a rare phenomenon, but when considered with other accounts of equally rare and bizarre human attributes, such as incombustibility, elongation and superhuman strength, it must be taken seriously. Mothers who lift cars off their trapped children, firewalkers and eaters and the sleepwalkers who perform 'impossible' feats pose profound questions about the nature of Man's physical and psychical potential. Perhaps we are intended to be able to defy gravity at will. Until we understand the nature of the phenomenon it must remain one of Man's mysterious hidden powers.

D.D. Home: flight from reality?

The pinnacle of D.D. Home's career came when he was seen to float out of one window and in through another

ONE OF THE MOST controversial events in the history of paranormal phenomena involved the most famous Victorian medium, Daniel Dunglas Home, who had never been detected in fraudulent activity during any of his 1500 recorded seances. This particular event, so special yet to many so suspicious, was Home's alleged levitation out of one window – some considerable distance from the ground – and back in through another. There were three witnesses to this bizarre incident: Lord Adare, his cousin Captain Charles Wynne, and the Master of Lindsay – all prominent and reputable members of London society. Yet the curious thing is that

Above: an artist's impression of Home levitating. Although his psychic talents included incombustibility, bodily elongation and the manifestation of apports, he was primarily famous for his spectacular levitations

those are the only details about this event that are known with any certainty. The classic – some would say credulous – account has already been given. The results of more penetrating and objective modern research are given space here.

On 13 December 1868 those three gentlemen met for a seance with Home in an apartment in the central London area. Even their accounts of where the incident took place differed. Lord Adare said 5 Buckingham Gate, Kensington; he also said in another account that it took place at Ashley Place, Westminster. Lindsay, however, favoured Victoria Street, Westminster.

Author, sceptic and debunker of the paranormal John Sladek lists other discrepancies among the witnesses' various statements in his book *The New Apocrypha*:

There was a ledge 4 inches [10 centimetres] wide below the windows (Adare); a ledge $1\frac{1}{2}$ inches [4 centimetres] wide (Lindsay); no foothold at all (Lindsay); balconies 7 feet [2 metres] apart (Adare); no balconies at all (Lindsay). The windows were 85 feet [25 metres] from the street (Lindsay); 70 feet [21 metres] (Lindsay); 80 feet [24 metres] (Home); on the third floor (Adare); on the first floor (Adare). It was dark (Adare); there was bright moonlight (Lindsay). Home was asleep in one room and the witnesses went into the next (Adare); Home left the witnesses in one room and went himself into the next (Adare).

In the footsteps of D.D. Home

Significantly, Captain Wynne's only recorded statement on the matter simply says: 'Home went out of one window and came in at another.' The word 'levitation' is conspicuous by its absence.

However, discrediting the witnesses by quoting the discrepancies in their statements does not necessarily imply the incident never took place. Nor have the conflicting addresses given proved too much of an obstacle in tracing the scene of the phenomenon. Archie Jarman, in his meticulously researched article published in *Alpha* magazine in October 1980, described how he managed to track down the house in question, using as his first reference *one* letter – written to Sir Francis Burnand by Lord Adare.

In this letter Adare states that the event took place at Ashley House, but gave it the wrong address, saying it was in Victoria Street. Archie Jarman noted:

The two rooms at Ashley House were connected by folding doors . . . The sash-windows opened onto stone balconies about 15 inches [38 centimetres] wide and running the width of the windows. Lord Lindsay later recorded that the balconies were 7 feet 5 inches [2 metres 13 centimetres] apart and it was this gap that Home was supposed to have crossed by means of levitation. An important clue given by Adare was that there was a 6-inch [15-centimetre] recess in the main wall of the building between the windows. Jarman walked the length of Victoria Street hoping to find a faded inscription on one of the older buildings that would reveal the real 'Ashley House', but he found nothing helpful and no one who knew of its existence. But he did find an 'Ashley Place' close to the precincts of Westminster Cathedral and one of its few remaining older buildings looked promising. This was 1–10 Ashley Place. The caretaker told Jarman of the building's chequered history since its construction in 1845; of the minor repairs carried out after a bomb had exploded close to it in 1944, and that the suites – residential in Home's time – were now offices. But more significant was the fact that it used to be called 'Ashley House' before the GPO changed it to 'Ashley Place' in 1930 for some reason of their own.

Teetering on the ledge

As Jarman says, 'seeing as Home had been flying high' he took the lift to the top floor, now occupied by a firm of architects. Rather surprisingly, perhaps, Mr Perry, one of the executives of the firm, did not think Mr Jarman a crank in his search for the suite where D. D. Home 'flew'. Indeed, he was most helpful. He showed Jarman that two of his rooms were, in fact, connected by folding doors as described in Adare's account.

Mr Perry and Archie Jarman measured the distance between the balconies – 7 feet 5 inches (2 metres 13 centimetres), confirming Lindsay's description and the 6-inch (15-centimetre) recess mentioned by Adare was also present. The drop to the ground was 45 feet (13.5 metres) – not quite the 80 feet (24 metres) claimed by Home, but still a long way to fall.

Jarman noticed an architectural feature not mentioned in any of the witnesses' accounts – a flat cornice, or ledge, about 5 inches (13 centimetres) wide, ran just below the balconies. Perhaps, after all, the irreproachable Home had edged his way along this narrow foothold from window to window, simply fulfilling Captain Wynne's baldly descriptive statement.

However, Mr Jarman was nothing if not courageous. With some help from the caretaker, and taking sensible precautions, he tried to make his own way along the ledge but soon gave up. It was impossible to cross between the balconies on that ledge.

Another explanation that occurred to Archie Jarman was that Home had perhaps walked a tightrope between the balconies, having previously strung a rope or cord between them and attached it to the old-fashioned pivot-bolt of the blinds, which would have protruded beyond the windows. Intrepidly, Jarman proposed to try this death-defying feat himself but the landlords

Right: Daniel Dunglas Home (1833–1886) was undoubtedly the most famous medium of all time. He claimed to be the love-child of a Scottish peer but was brought up modestly in the United States by an aunt

Above: Home was often the butt of cartoonists. His spectacular feats brought him wealth and fame; but critics accused him of being a fraud and a gold-digger and his close friendship with Lord Adare was whispered to be 'unnatural'. The press made the most of Home's legal adoption by a rich old lady, and the fact that he fled from her when her attentions became more than motherly

refused to sanction such a dangerous 're-construction'. However, it seems likely that Home could have faked his *pièce de résistance* by some artificial means such as tightrope-walking, or even swinging, Tarzan-like, between balconies.

Jarman's suspicions had been aroused by two unusual conditions surrounding the 'levitation' on the evening of 13 December 1868. One was Home's insistence that he *would* 'levitate' out of a specific window and back in through another. Yet this was the very medium who often remarked that he had no control over the 'spirits' who, he believed, raised him up. So why put them to the test with 45 feet (13.5 metres) of thin air and a stony pavement beneath him?

Jarman draws our attention to a second suspicious factor. Before his exit from the window Home made the three witnesses promise not to move from their chairs until he re-emerged. When he reappeared he thanked them for their co-operation in this matter. But if they had rushed to the window what would they have seen, what would their presence have ruined? The powers of the spirits? Home's concentration as he walked the tightrope or swung from balcony to balcony? Home's entire reputation once and for all? We shall never know, for like the noble English gentlemen they were, they kept their promise and remained seated, well away from the window. They saw him go out of one window and come in through another. That is all they saw.

And yet hundreds of people had witnessed Home levitate in drawing rooms in America and all over Europe. There was no doubt in their minds that the levitations they witnessed were totally genuine, inexplicable phenomena. It would be very sad if Home's only deliberate cheating was on the occasion of his most famous 'triumph'.

Ashes to ashes

Of all the strange and inexplicable fates that may befall a person, perhaps the most bizarre is to burst into flames without warning and without apparent cause. BOB RICKARD describes cases that still defy science

PEOPLE HAVE LONG BELIEVED that in certain circumstances the human body can burst into flames of its own accord. Flames, furthermore, of such ferocity that within minutes the victim is reduced to a heap of carbonised ashes. This idea – some call it a superstition – has been around for centuries, smouldering in the belief in divine retribution. 'By the blast of God they perish,' says the author of *Job*, 'and by the breath of his nostrils are they consumed.'

This Gothic horror was hugely popular in the 18th and 19th centuries, and its literary use is still extensively discussed in the pages of *The Dickensian*, stimulated by Charles Dickens' own fascination with the subject. Dickens had examined the case for spontaneous human combustion (SHC) 'as a Judge might have done', and knew most of the early authorities and collections of cases. He probably based his description of Krook's death

The aftermath of spontaneous human combustion. The fire has reduced most of the body to ashes, leaving only parts of the lower legs, the left hand and portions of the skull, and was intense enough to burn a hole in the floor. Enormously high temperatures must have been involved, yet for some mysterious reason the fire has been contained, causing little further damage to the surroundings

in *Bleak House* (1852–3), upon the cases of Countess Bandi and Grace Pett.

The death of the 62-year-old Countess Cornelia Bandi, near Verona, is perhaps one of the first of the more reliable reports of SHC. According to a statement by Bianchini, a prebendary of Verona, dated 4 April 1731, the Countess had been put to bed after supper, and fell asleep after several hours' conversation with her maid. In the morning the maid returned to wake her and found a grisly scene. As the *Gentlemen's Magazine* reported: 'The floor of the chamber was thick-smear'd with a gluish moisture, not easily got off . . . and from the lower part of the window trickl'd down a greasy, loathsome, yellowish liquor with an unusual stink.'

Specks of soot hung in the air and covered all the surfaces in the room, and the smell had penetrated adjoining rooms. The bed was undamaged, the sheets turned back, indicating the Countess had got out of bed.

Four feet [1.3 metres] from the bed was a heap of ashes, two legs untouch'd, stockings on, between which lay the head, the brains, half of the back-part of the skull and the whole chin burn'd to ashes, among which were found three fingers blacken'd. All the rest was ashes which had this quality, that they left in the hand a greasy and stinking moisture.

A hole burnt in the floor

Bianchini could have been describing some of our modern cases. The diligent researches of Larry E. Arnold unearthed the fate of Dr J. Irving Bentley, a 93-year-old retired physician of Coudersport, Pennsylvania. Gas company worker Don Gosnell discovered the remains after smelling a 'light-blue smoke of unusual odor'. The fire had been so intense that it almost totally consumed the old man. John Dec the deputy coroner said: 'All I found was a knee joint atop a post in the basement, the lower leg from the knee down, and the now-scattered ashes 6 feet [2 metres] below.' And yet the fire had, mysteriously, been contained; firemen testified to the existence of a few embers around the hole, and a slight scorching on the bathtub about a foot (30 centimetres) away was the only other sign of this fiercely fatal fire. The burns on the bath were still visible when Arnold investigated nine years later.

It was suggested that Bentley was a careless smoker – small burns riddled his everyday clothes and the bedroom floor – and that he had wakened to find himself on fire, struggled to the bathroom in search of water, and there collapsed and died. Arnold, in his report on the case in the journal *Pursuit*, 1976, points out that there are several inconsistencies in this account, though it was accepted by the local newspaper and the coroner.

Bentley's pipe had been 'carefully placed' on its stand by his chair; not the action of a man on fire. A broken hip six years before had left him with no feeling in his left leg, and he walked with difficulty – his 'walker' can be seen fallen across the hole. He was enough of a doctor to realise that his only chance of survival, had his clothes been on fire, would be to take them off there and then, rather than risk the precarious trip to the bathroom.

It is more likely that whatever happened to Bentley occurred when he visited the bathroom for some other reason, and that he was beginning to burn before he took off his robe, setting fire to it in the process – it was found smouldering in the bathtub. The autopsy was a mere formality, yet despite having so little to go on – just half a leg; the ashes

A villain meets his end

In chapter 32 of *Bleak House*, Charles Dickens' characters, William Guppy and Tony Weevle, discover that the evil Krook has been mysteriously burned to a few charred lumps and ashes, filling the room with 'hateful soot' and objects coated with an offensive 'thick yellow liquor'. 'Call the death by any name . . . attribute it to whom you will, or say it might have been prevented how you will, it is the same death eternally – inborn, inbred, engendered in the corrupt humours of the vicious body itself, and that only – Spontaneous Combustion, and none other of all the deaths that can be died.'

were never analysed – the coroner decided that Dr Bentley had died of *asphyxiation*, probably because that is the usual cause of death during fires.

Primarily due to the efforts of Charles Fort, the pioneer collector of accounts of strange phenomena, and the small number of people and journals who continue his work, we have accumulated a respectable number of records, from newspapers and medical journals, of SHC right up to the present. Very few of the accounts mention SHC, because officially there is no such phenomenon, and coroners and their advisers have the unenviable task of dealing with evidence that seems to contradict accepted physical laws and medical opinion. Inevitably, suppositions are made about knocked over heaters, flying sparks, careless smoking, and in the case of child victims, playing with matches. Faced with the alternative – a nightmare out of the Dark Ages – it is not surprising that they are accepted.

There are occasional exceptions, which are far more useful to those who truly wish to solve the enigma, like the report in *Lloyds Weekly News* of 5 February 1905. A woman asleep by a fireplace woke to find herself in flames and later died. The honest coroner said he could not understand: the woman had gone to sleep facing the fire, so any cinder that shot out from the grate would ignite the front of her clothes. Yet it was her back that bore the severe burns.

Fear of the truth

At worst, a story may be rejected out of fear or disbelief, as in the case of the elderly spinster, Wilhelmina Dewar, who combusted near midnight on 22 March 1908, in the Northumberland town of Whitley Bay. Wilhelmina was found by her sister Margaret who, in a shocked state, managed to summon her neighbours. In the house they found the severely charred body of Wilhelmina in an upstairs bed. The bedclothes were unscorched and there was no sign of fire anywhere else in the house.

When Margaret told this story at the inquest, the coroner thought it preposterous and asked her to think again. Repeatedly she said she was telling the truth and could not change her story – even after a policeman testified that Margaret was so drunk she couldn't have known what she was saying. As Fort points out, the policeman 'was not called upon to state how he distinguished between signs of excitement and terror, and intoxication.' The coroner adjourned the inquest to give her more time to think. When it was reconvened a few days later it was obvious that a great deal of pressure had been placed upon poor Margaret.

Both sisters were retired school teachers and, up until then, lived respectably. Now the coroner was calling her a liar, the papers called her a drunk, and friends and neighbours turned away, leaving her to face a hostile court. Not surprisingly, she said she had been inaccurate. This time she told a story of finding her sister burned, but alive, in a lower part of the house. Then she helped her upstairs to bed, where she died.

This sounded superficially more plausible, was accepted, and the proceedings promptly closed. The court was not interested in how Wilhelmina was transformed from someone who could be helped upstairs into the cindered corpse with charred abdomen and legs; or how, if she continued to smoulder after being helped into bed, there was no mark of fire in the house. 'But the coroner was satisfied,' wrote Fort sarcastically. 'The proper testimony had been recorded.'

Yet it was medico-legal interest that kept alive the notion of SHC, with pathologists endorsing the phenomenon, than rejecting it in favour of 'preternatural combustibility'. In addition, there was the perennial possibility that a murderer may simulate SHC to hide his crime. One of the earliest test cases occurred in Rheims in 1725 when an innkeeper, Jean Millet, was accused of having an affair with a pretty servant girl and killing his wife. The wife, who was often drunk, was found one morning about a foot (30 centimetres) away from the hearth.

'A part of the head only, with a portion of the lower extremities, and a few of the vertebrae, had escaped combustion. A foot and a half (45 centimetres) of the flooring under the body had been consumed, but a kneading-trough and a powdering tub very near the body sustained no injury.' A young assistant doctor, named Le Cat, was staying at the inn and managed to convince the court that this was no ordinary fire death but a 'visitation of God' upon the drunken woman, and an obvious result of soaking one's innards with spirits. Millet was vindicated, and Le Cat went on to qualify with distinction, and publish a memoir on SHC.

Spontaneous human combustion received its severest criticism from the great pioneer chemist, Baron Justus von Liebig, who wrote a spirited refutation of both spontaneous and preternatural combustion, on the grounds that no one had seen it happen. As a scientist he saw the historical evidence as an unsupported record of the *belief* in SHC, rather than actual proof of spontaneous burning deaths. Further, he lamented the lack of expert witnesses, and dismissed the accounts generally because they 'proceed from ignorant persons, unpractised in observation, and bear in themselves the stamp of untrustworthiness.'

Despite Liebig's assertion, however, there is plenty of evidence from both medical and police sources. Many of these bear witness to the ferocity of the phenomenon, as in the case investigated by Merille, a surgeon in Caen, recorded in Trotter's *Essay on drunkenness* (1804). On 3 June 1782, Merille was asked by 'the king's officers' in the city to report on the death of Mademoiselle Thaurs, a lady of over 60 who had been observed, that day, to have drunk three bottles of wine and one of brandy. Merille wrote:

The body lay with the crown of the head resting against one of the handirons . . . 18 inches [45 centimetres] from the fire, the remainder of the body was placed obliquely before the chimney, the whole being nothing but a mass of ashes. Even the most solid bones had lost their form and consistence. The right foot was found entire and scorched at its upper junction; the left was more burnt. The day was cold but there was nothing in the grate except two or three bits of wood about an inch in diameter, burnt in the middle.

Dr Wilton Krogman, who investigated a famous case of SHC, and experimented with

Left: the great chemist Baron Justus von Liebig. He rejected tales of spontaneous human combustion because of the lack of expert witnesses – and because his attempts to make flesh burn with the same intensity as SHC were, without exception, a dismal failure

Below: an anonymous victim of SHC lies with its apparently unburnt head resting in a grate. An electric fire is also visible – but how did the body burn so thoroughly without setting fire to the rest of the room?

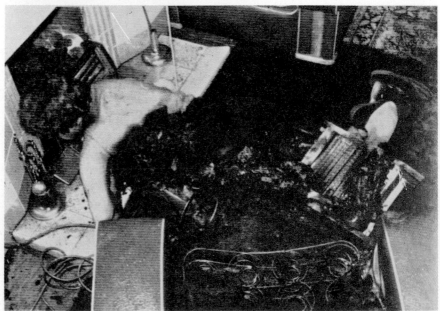

The burning of Dr Bentley

Dr J. Irving Bentley, a retired physician, lived on the ground floor of an apartment building in Coudersport, northern Pennsylvania. On the cold morning of 5 December 1966, Don Gosnell entered the building's basement to read the meter for the North Pen Gas Company. In the basement a 'light-blue smoke of unusual odor' hung in the air. Scattering an unfamiliar heap in the corner with his boot, Gosnell found it was ashes. There had been no answer to his greeting on the way in, so he decided to look in on the old man. There was more strange smoke in the bedroom but no sign of Bentley. Gosnell peered into the bathroom and was confronted with a sight he will never forget. A large hole had burned through the floor to the basement, exposing the joists and pipework below. On the edge of the hole he saw '. . . a brown leg from the knee down, like that of a mannequin. I didn't look further!' Gosnell fled from the building.

sophisticated crematorium equipment, said: 'Only at 3000°F (1500°C) plus have I seen bone fuse or melt so that it ran and became volatile.' Such a heat would certainly char everything within a considerable radius and set the house ablaze, yet the meticulous Merille writes:

> None of the furniture in the apartment was damaged. The chair on which she was sitting was found at the distance of a foot from her, and absolutely untouched . . . the consumption of the body had taken place in less than 7 hours, though according to appearance, nothing around the body was burnt but the clothes.

Reluctant admissions

Modern researchers into SHC readily quash the idea that the phenomenon is as rare as some commentators suggest. Similarly, there is a growing number of cases testified to by doctors and pathologists, and this number would probably increase if the fear of ridicule could be completely removed. A Dr B. H. Hartwell reported to the Massachusetts Medico-Legal Society an unusual case of SHC that he witnessed while driving through Ayer, Massachusetts, on 12 May 1890.

He was stopped and called into a wood where he saw a horrible sight. In a clearing a woman was crouching 'in flames at the shoulders, both sides of the abdomen, and both legs.' Neither he nor the other witnesses could find an obvious cause for the fire.

This doctor's experience was not unique. Support for the suspicion that many a doctor would be able to tell of an encounter with mysterious and fatal fires comes in a coincidental and roundabout way. Maxwell Cade and Delphine Davis, authors of the imaginative study of ball lightning *Taming of the thunderbolts* (1969), confessed they themselves would not have put much faith in the above story, or in the existence of SHC, 'if a doctor friend had not told us of a lecture which he attended at the Massachusetts Medico-Legal Society, where several such cases were discussed. When we expressed cautious doubts, the doctor assured us that he had been called to a similar case himself as recently as the autumn of 1959.'

When Dr D. J. Gee of the University of Leeds delivered his well-known paper on 'A case of spontaneous combustion' he was surprised by the candid discussion that followed. He is quoted as saying:

> Dr George Manning described his experience of several similar cases, and indicated that the phenomenon was certainly not as rare as might be supposed from the literature. This view was supported by Dr David Price, who said that he met with this phenomenon approximately once in every four years.

A strange unnatural fire

The idea that human beings can burst into flames of their own accord is odd enough. But, as BOB RICKARD shows, everything about spontaneous human combustion is bizarre

Spontaneous human combustion strikes with astonishing speed, yet the heat generated is sufficient to char even the bones of the victim. In contrast, a body can take hours to burn away in the sustained fire of a crematorium – and even then only the flesh is thoroughly destroyed

PERHAPS THE MOST common characteristic of SHC is the sheer speed with which it strikes. Many victims were seen alive only a few moments before the fire struck from nowhere. An Italian surgeon called Battaglio reported the death of a priest, named Bertholi, in the town of Filetto, in 1789. Lodging with his brother-in-law, he had been left alone in his room reading a prayerbook. A few minutes later he screamed. People came running to find him on the floor surrounded by a pale flame, which receded as they approached.

Bertholi wore a sackcloth under his clothes, next to his skin, and it was immediately apparent that the outer clothes had burned away leaving the sackcloth intact. Under the sackcloth the skin on the man's trunk was not burned, but detached from the flesh and hung in shreds.

Some writers deduce that the fire develops with particular rapidity, from the fact that the victims are often discovered still sitting calmly, as though nothing had happened.

A dramatic example is given in Ron Willis's article on SHC in *INFO Journal* 8 (1972). In 1960, five charred bodies were found in a burned-out car near Pikeville, Kentucky. The coroner commented: 'They were sitting there as though they'd just gotten into the car. With all that heat it seems there'd be some sort of struggle to escape. But there hadn't been.'

Another almost universal characteristic of SHC is the extreme intensity of heat that is involved. Under normal circumstances the human body is very hard to set alight, especially if still alive, and people who die in fires usually sustain only partial or superficial damage to the body. Reduction to a pile of calcined ashes, experts all agree, demands a fierce heat which needs to be externally fuelled and maintained for hours, and even so crematoria still have to grind up the bones that remain afterward.

The death of Mrs Reeser (see box) was investigated by Dr Wilton M. Krogman, a renowned forensic anthropologist from the University of Pennsylvania School of Medicine, who has researched and experimented the causes and effects of deaths by and during fires. He said he has watched bodies in a crematorium burn for over 8 hours at 2000°F (1110°C) without any sign of the bones becoming ashes or powder; and that it takes a heat of about 3000°F (1650°C) to make bone melt and become volatile. Willis mentions the case of Leon Eveille, aged 40, found burnt to a crisp in his locked car at Arcis-sur-Aube, France, on 17 June 1971. The heat had melted the windows. It was estimated that a burning car normally reaches about 1300°F (700°C), but to melt glass the temperature must have been over 1800°F (1000°C).

Time and again in cases of SHC, we encounter a further strange effect: the confinement of the heat. Charred bodies are found lying in unscorched beds, sitting on slightly singed chairs, or with their clothing intact.

In 1905 the *British Medical Journal* reported the death of 'an elderly woman of intemperate habits'. Authorities broke into a house from which smoke was issuing to find

a small pyramidal heap of broken calcinated human bones, on the top of

Dr Wilton Krogman, an expert on the effects of fire on the human body. He was astonished by the state of Mrs Reeser's corpse, and constructed an elaborate theory to account for it

which was a skull, on the floor in front of a chair. All the bones were completely bleached and brittle; every particle of soft tissue had been consumed, and yet a tablecloth within three feet of the remains was not even scorched. . . . Curiously, the ceiling was scorched, as if the woman had become a pillar of fire.

Fort, in his *Complete books* (1941) gives two startling cases. The first, from the *Daily News* of 17 December 1904, describes how Mrs Thomas Cochrane, of Falkirk, was found in a bedroom burned to death 'beyond recognition'. There had been no outcry, and little else burned, with no fire in the grate. Her charred corpse was found 'sitting in a chair, surrounded by pillows and cushions'. The second is from the *Madras Mail* of 13 May 1907 concerning a woman in the village of Manner, near Dinapore. Flames had consumed her body, but not her clothes. Two constables had found the corpse in a room in which nothing else showed signs of fire, and had carried the smouldering body to the District Magistrate.

In 1841 the *British Medical Journal* reported an address by Dr F. S. Reynolds to the Manchester Pathological Society on the subject of SHC. Although rejecting the idea of 'spontaneous' combustion, he admitted there were baffling cases, and gave an instance from his experience of a woman of 40 who fell near a hearth. She was found next morning still burning. What astonished him was the damage to the legs: inside unharmed stockings her femora were carbonised and knee-joints opened.

Some chroniclers of SHC have drawn attention to the lack of outcry and struggle by victims. 'In their grim submission,' Fort wrote, 'it is almost as if they had been lulled by the wings of a vampire.' There is more to it than being overcome by drink and fumes – some psychic or psychological component of the phenomenon prefaces or accompanies the burning, and this may explain the lack of escape, and the inability of surviving victims to tell what happened to them.

For example, the *Hull Daily Mail* of 6 January 1905 describes how an elderly

The destruction of Mary Reeser

Workmen are seen here clearing away the remains of the chair in which Mrs Mary Reeser, a widow of 67, of St Petersburg, Florida, departed this life on a pillar of fire, during the night of 1 July 1951. Damage to the surroundings was minimal. The overstuffed chair was burned down to its springs, there was a patch of soot on the ceiling above and a small circle of carpet was charred around the chair, but a pile of papers nearby was unscorched. Dr Wilton Krogman, a forensic scientist who specialised in fire deaths, was visiting in the area and joined the investigation. He said:

I cannot conceive of such complete cremation without more burning of the apartment itself. In fact the apartment and everything in it should have been consumed. Never have I seen a human skull shrunk by intense heat. The opposite has always been true; the skulls have been either abnormally swollen or have virtually exploded into hundreds of pieces . . . I regard it as the most amazing thing I have ever seen. As I review it, the short hairs on my neck bristle with vague fear. Were I living in the Middle Ages, I'd mutter something about black magic.

Police considered every likely theory, and a few unasked-for ideas from cranky members of the public: suicide by petrol, ignition of methane gas in her body, murder by flame-thrower, 'atomic pill' (whatever that meant), magnesium, phosphorus and napalm substances . . . and even a 'ball of fire' which one anonymous letter-writer claimed to see. In the end the coroner accepted the FBI theory, that she had fallen asleep while smoking and set her clothes alight.

Dr Krogman himself proffered the idea that Mrs Reeser had been burned elsewhere by someone with access to crematorium-type equipment or materials, then was carried back to the apartment, where the mystery assailant had added the finishing touches, like heat-buckled plastic objects, and a door-knob that was still hot in the morning. A year later, the police confessed the case was still open.

woman, Elizabeth Clark, was found in the morning with fatal burns, while her bed, in the Trinity Almshouse, Hull, was unmarked by fire. There had been no outcry or sounds of struggle through the thin partitions. She was 'unable to give an articulate account' of her accident, and later died. Of course that could mean that the authorities – not for the first time – simply didn't believe her account.

In *Lo!* (1930), Fort describes the complex fires that plagued Binbrook Farm, near Grimsby, in the winter of 1904–5. One incident involved a young servant girl who was burning without her knowledge, and might have been another SHC statistic had not her employer roused her from her day-dreaming (or trance). According to a local newspaper, the farmer said:

> Our servant girl, whom we had taken from the workhouse . . . was sweeping the kitchen. There was a very small fire in the grate; there was a guard there so that no one can come within 2 feet [0.6 metres] or more of the fire, and she was at the other end of the room, and had not been near. I suddenly came into the kitchen and there she was, sweeping away while the back of her dress was on fire. She looked around as I shouted, and seeing the flames, rushed through the door. She tripped and I smothered the fire out with wet sacks.

The girl had obviously been on fire for some time and was 'terribly burned'.

As we have seen in the Pikeville car case,

several people have combusted together, but such cases are extremely rare. Baron Liebig thought that the occurrence of multiple SHC cases disproved the 'disease' theory (see box), since in his experience a disease has never run the same course in two or more people, detail for detail, culminating in their simultaneous death. Certainly none of the 'diseases' that are suggested by the theory's apologists has done so.

Willis describes the case of the Rooneys who lived in a farmhouse near Seneca, Illinois:

> On Christmas Eve 1885, Patrick Rooney and his wife and their hired man, John Larson, were drinking whiskey in the kitchen. Larson went to bed and woke up Christmas morning feeling sick. Downstairs in the kitchen he found everything covered with an oily film, and on the floor, Patrick Rooney dead. Larson rode to get help from Rooney's son John, who lived nearby. Back at the farm the two men noticed that there was a charred hole next to the kitchen table. Looking into the hole they found, on the earth under the kitchen floor, a calcined skull, a few charred bones and a pile of ashes. Mrs Rooney had been obliterated by a fantastically hot fire that had not spread beyond her immediate area.

The coroner soon found that Patrick had been suffocated by the smoke of the burning body of his wife.

Charles Fort, who spent a lifetime collecting reports of SHC and other inexplicable occurrences. Fort wondered if SHC might be connected with demonology: 'I think our data relate not to "spontaneous combustion of human bodies" but to things or beings, that with a flaming process consume men and women, but like werewolves or alleged werewolves, mostly pick women.'

Fuelling the human fireball

Among the early pathologists the theory arose that in certain circumstances the body may produce gases that combust on exposure to quantities of oxygen. The distinguished scientist Baron Karl von Reichenbach wrote of the 'miasma of putrefaction' of human bodies, for instance. But Liebig could find no evidence of such a gas, 'in health, in disease, nay not even in the putrefaction of dead bodies.'

Dixon Mann and W. A. Brend, in their *Forensic medicine and toxicology* (1914) give the case of a fat man who died two hours after admission to Guy's Hospital, London, in 1885. The following day his corpse was found bloated, the skin distended all over and filled with gas, although there was no sign of decomposition. 'When punctures were made in the skin, the gas escaped and burnt with a flame like that of carburetted hydrogen; as many as a dozen flames were burning at the same time.' Had the man died at home near a fire, another case of 'spontaneous combustion' would have been reported to confuse researchers further.

However, gases within the body tissues of the sort suggested would be fatally toxic, and the victim would have been gravely ill or dead. And generally there are no such symptoms: victims have often been seen alive shortly before their flaming. Nor does this theory account for the observed fact of clothes that are left unburnt on a charred corpse.

As an alternative to the disease theory, we might consider organic or mechanical malfunctions of normal processes within the body. Ivan Sanderson and, before him, Vincent Gaddis, speculated about the build-up of phosphagens in muscle tissue, particularly the vitamin B10, vital to normal energy supplies. A technical paper in *Applied Trophology* (December 1957) included this relevant paragraph:

> Phosphagen is a compound like nitro-glycerine, of endothermic formation. It is no doubt so highly developed in certain sedentary persons as to make their bodies actually combustible, subject to ignition, burning like wet gunpowder under some circumstances.

This may explain the readiness of some bodies to blaze, but we still have to identify the source of ignition.

An unmistakable case of simultaneous SHC is summarised by Fort, of an elderly couple named Kiley, who lived near Southampton. On the morning of 26 February 1905, neighbours heard a curious 'scratching' and went next door to investigate. They entered the house and found it in flames inside. Kiley was found burned to death on the floor. Mrs Kiley, burned to death, was sitting in a chair in the same room, 'badly charred but recognisable'. Both bodies were fully dressed,

> judging by the fragments of clothes, indicating they had been burned before their time for going to bed . . . the mystery was that two persons, neither of whom had cried for help, presumably not asleep in any ordinary sense, should have been burned to death in a fire that did not manifest as a general fire until hours later.

There are on record two cases of SHC which coincided with suicide attempts, the implication of which is obscure unless one presupposes some form of the 'psychic suicide' theory in which victims combust because they have given up on life.

On 13 December 1959, 27-year-old Billy Peterson, of Pontiac, Michigan, said goodbye to his mother and drove to his garage where he hooked a pipe from the car's exhaust into the car itself. Only 40 minutes after Billy had left his mother, a passing motorist saw the smoke and investigated. Inside the car Billy was dead from carbon monoxide poisoning, but it was the condition of his body that puzzled pathologists. His back, arms and legs were covered in third-degree burns, and some parts of him were charred to a crisp. Despite all this, his clothes and underclothes were quite unharmed.

On 18 September 1952, Glen Denney, 46, a foundry worker in Louisiana, cut the arteries in his left arm and both wrists and ankles, but he had died from inhaling smoke. When found, he was a 'mass of flames' with nothing else in the room ablaze. The coroner guessed that he had poured kerosene over himself and lit a match, though no container was found, and just how he could hold, let alone light, a match with arterial blood pumping over his hands at about 4 per cent of body volume per second was not explained. The investigator, Otto Burma, wrote: 'There is no doubt in my mind that Denney did in fact attempt suicide. But while in the process of carrying out this act his body caught fire due to some unknown cause.'

Many other aspects of SHC would reward investigation. There are, for instance, demonstrable connections with poltergeist phenomena, which frequently involve mysterious spontaneous fires. Then there are people who are fire-prone, in whose presence fires repeatedly break out. Examining these and other facts that surround SHC may lead us nearer to understanding the phenomenon – and perhaps to identifying its causes.

The end of an old soldier

On 19 February 1888, Dr J. Mackenzie Booth, a lecturer at Aberdeen University, was called to the loft of a stable in Constitution Street, where he found the

charred corpse of a 65-year-old pensioner. There was considerable damage to the body: most of the fleshy parts had burned away exposing the calcined ends of bones. The floor around the man had burnt through so that the corpse rested on a charred beam. The heat had also burned the roofing slats above him, causing some slates to fall onto his chest and damage his brittle form further. He was last seen going into the loft with a bottle and lamp the previous evening.

It was thought that he had knocked the lamp over and then been overcome by drink and smoke. (Booth's report describes the 'old soldier' as being 'of inebriate habits'.) But the lamp had been seen to go out shortly after he went into the loft, and no fire was seen during the night. Furthermore, it is clear from this engraving (from the *British Medical Journal* of 21 April 1888, and based directly on a photograph of the scene) that the bales of hay surrounding the man did not catch fire. The carbonised face retained recognisable features, from which, and from 'the comfortably recumbent attitude of the body' Booth noted that 'it was evident that there had been no death struggle.'

Mysteries of the human bonfire

Medical men and scientists have long doubted that spontaneous human combustion actually occurs. But the facts stubbornly refuse to fit their conventional explanations

DEATHS THAT APPEAR to have been caused by spontaneous human combustion (SHC) have always been an embarrassment to the medical profession. The refusal to believe in SHC is not the result of a deliberate conspiracy to suppress the evidence, however. Rather there has been a turning away, a wish not to think about such an outrage of accepted medical and scentific knowledge.

If SHC is mentioned at all, it is only to be dismissed as a belief mistakenly held by the uninformed, or as a superstition lingering from less enlightened times. J. L. Casper, for example, in his *Handbook of the practice of forensic medicine*, complained: 'It is sad to think that in an earnest scientific work, in this year of grace 1861, we must still treat of the fable of "spontaneous combustion".' And opinion today is hardly less compromising. Dr Gavin Thurston, the coroner for Inner West London, has said that 'no such phenomenon as spontaneous combustion exists, or has ever occurred'.

At the same time, those scientists and doctors who have examined the effects closely, acknowledge that there have been cases of death by burning that are genuinely inexplicable. But since SHC officially does not exist, some other reason has had to be found for the same effects. And so the notion of 'preternatural combustibility' was born.

The next step was to identify the causes of such a combustibility – and, in any given case, to discover its source of ignition. So, in the middle of the 19th century, a typical SHC victim was thought to be almost certainly a drinker and a smoker; most likely an elderly, solitary, corpulent woman of sedentary habits. Alcohol was both the physical and the moral cause of conflagration. Horrific tales circulated about divine punishment for inebriation, in which the lambent and inextinguishable flames were but a foretaste of the everlasting hellfire to come. Boineau, a French priest, reported the 1749 case of an 80-year-old woman reduced to a carbonised skeleton as she sat sipping brandy. As Baron Justus von Liebig noted sarcastically, 'The chair, which of course had not sinned, did not burn.'

Liebig, in fact, sceptical of SHC though he was, utterly discredited the notion that there was any connection between the phenomenon and drinking. Liebig showed conclusively that alcohol-saturated flesh will burn only until the alcohol is used up; and fatty tissue behaves in the same way – when it can be set alight.

In his 1965 article in *Medicine, science and the law*, Dr D. J. Gee, a lecturer in forensic

Top: Only the legs remain of Mrs E.M., a widow who died on 29 January 1958. Was she burnt by the fire in the grate, or did she combust of her own accord?

Above: Dr Gavin Thurston, who has firmly stated that SHC has never taken place

medicine at Leeds University, described his own experiments following his examination of a charred corpse in 1963. Dr Gee successfully, set light to small quantities of fat, but the burning could be sustained only by placing the sample in a strong draught. Even this resulted in no more than a slow smouldering, not the spectacular blaze typical of SHC. However, this has only made it necessary for investigators of what would otherwise be admitted as cases of SHC to look for the 'explanatory' sustaining draught, and prompted some writers to highlight victims who were found in or near a fireplace, where there would be such an updraught.

The readiness with which coroners have adopted these suggestions seems to indicate a strong desire to terminate the proceedings as quickly, conveniently and 'reasonably' as possible, rather than admit a bizarre and frightening mystery. Some verdicts are far from satisfactory. Consider the case of Grace Pett, a fishwife of Ipswich, who was found on the morning of 10 April 1744, lying on the floor near the grate, and burning 'like a block of wood . . . with a glowing fire without flame'. After the fire was put out, Grace was seen to be 'like a heap of charcoal covered with white ashes'. That Grace was a regular smoker, and had the previous evening 'drunk plentifully of gin' in welcoming a daughter

home from Gibraltar, were sufficient for the advocates of temperance and preternatural combustibility.

There are several details in this case, however, that afford these apologists no comfort. According to the account in Sir David Brewster's *Natural magic* (1842) there had been no fire at all in the grate, and a candle, in use that fateful evening, had burnt down safely overnight in its candlestick. And worse: 'The clothes of a child on one side of her, and a paper screen on the other were untouched', and the wooden floor beneath her burning body 'was neither singed nor discoloured'.

Can we, in the 20th century, offer an alternative explanation for SHC besides 'preternatural combustibility'? The savants of the 19th century can be forgiven for thinking only in terms of conventional fire. But since the admirable Liebig's day the physical and medical sciences have made enormous progress. Today we know of many forms of death that can penetrate a man's body silently and invisibly. Military research into 'radiation weapons' has supplemented nuclear radiation with beamed ultrasound, x-ray lasers, microwave projectors and other horrors, all of which can cook a man inside his clothes. But the spirit of Liebig exhorts us to be rigorous: even if we credit the idea of an

Sir David Brewster, whose account of one fire death bears all the marks of a case of SHC. The coroner, however, thought otherwise

A burning rage

Reviewing the cases of SHC in his book *Mysterious fires and lights* (1967), veteran Fortean Vincent Gaddis noted that a high proportion of victims had apparently given up on life. 'Some were alcoholics, and alcoholism is a form of escape from reality . . . Most were elderly with lowered resistance and perhaps tired of life. Many were invalids or poverty-stricken, dying in rest homes or almshouses. Many led idle, sedentary lives.' Charles Fort and his successors have also observed a significant number of 'no-hopers' among SHC victims. In *Fire from heaven* Michael Harrison suggests that

there are several kinds of SHC, one of which is self-induced by people who are depressed, lonely, deprived, frightened and perhaps resentful. Harrison wonders if normally controlled reserves of physical and psychical energy are not suddenly released in a fatal conflagration, as a kind of 'psychic suicide'.

Suicide by fire has always had symbolic overtones, and has been used to make a political gesture. That a massive build-up of rage or despair may result in a spontaneous blaze is appealing, but it is highly conjectural. Besides, it would account for only some cases.

ubiquitous madman recently on the loose with a death ray, we still have to account for the instances from the past.

There are in fact a number of theories that might account for SHC, though not all are equally attractive. Among the least likely are the 'psychic suicide' theory (see box), and the proposition that people whose clothes are set alight catch fire themselves.

This was the suggestion in the case of Phyllis Newcombe. At midnight on 27 August 1938 she and her fiancé were leaving the dance floor of a Chelmsford ballroom, when she suddenly screamed. Her crinoline dress had become a mass of flames. It was put out with some difficulty – and too late, for Phyllis died in hospital a few hours later. At the inquest it was suggested that a discarded cigarette had set the dress alight. The material flamed when a lighter was put to it, but failed to catch fire when lit cigarettes were thrown at it. The coroner expressed his puzzlement and gave a verdict of accidental death. Puzzled he might have been, since in any case external fires cannot produce burns as extensive as those in SHC cases unless large quantities of fuel and oxygen are supplied over a considerable period of time. Even when these conditions are met, the body is burnt from the outside *in*. But there are many cases of SHC in which the burning takes place *within* the flesh, and the clothes or surroundings remain unharmed.

Another somewhat unsatisfactory thesis is the 'corrosive liquid' theory, and it likewise attempts to explain *away* certain cases of death by fire. Nevertheless this was the reason suggested for the death of Madge Knight. At about 3.30 a.m. on 19 November

The scorching of a slim lady

Photographic evidence of bizarre burning deaths is very rare and not readily accessible even to the dedicated and bona fide researcher. The charred remains shown here are of 'a slim lady, 85 years old, who was in good health' when she was consumed by flames in November 1963. The case was investigated by Dr D. J. Gee. Because of extensive damage to the body (but to little else) it was assumed that the victim had been in a state of unusual combustibility, and was set alight by an ember or a spark – a theory that would accord with the results of Dr Gee's experiments and the theory of preternatural combustibility.

Conflagration of a clergyman

While away from his parish in Stockcross, Newbury, England, the Reverend Mr Adams burned to death in a hotel room in New York, in 1876, apparently as a result of spontaneous combustion. In *Fire from heaven*, Michael Harrison remarks that 'ecclesiastics, as a class' seem strangely vulnerable to SHC and other paranormal heat phenomena.

1943 she was asleep alone in the spare room of her house in Aldingbourne, Sussex. She awoke feeling as if she were on fire. Her screams brought her husband and others who were sharing the house.

Madge was naked under the bedclothes, but she was in agony because extensive burning had removed most of the skin from her back. A doctor administered morphine, and, bemused, called in a Harley Street specialist. The specialist later told the coroner that he thought the burns must have been caused by a corrosive liquid because there was no sign of fire on the sheets or anywhere else in the room, and no smell of burning. Madge was repeatedly questioned but could not, or would not, say what had happened before she died in hospital in Chichester, on 6 December.

The lack of any sign of fire in many cases has led some researchers to theorise about substances that can burn without flame. In Madge Knight's case, no trace of any corrosive chemical could be found, nor any possible container for it. The notion that Madge hid the evidence before crawling into bed is too absurd to contemplate.

Perhaps the most fruitful clue to the

nature of the phenomenon came in 1975, with Livingstone Gearhart's article in the Fortean journal *Pursuit*. He had discovered that a significant number of SHC cases took place on or near a peak in the geomagnetic flux. The strength of the Earth's magnetic field rises and falls quite dramatically in relation to solar activity. Global averages of the daily figures are gathered for astronomers and geophysicists, and these show a distinct correlation between the incidence of SHC and high geomagnetic readings. This seems to indicate that SHC may be the result of a very complex chain of events, in which there is an interaction between certain astronomical conditions and the state of an individual's body. These in turn form the preconditions for the 'ball lightning' theory.

Ball lightning has been offered as one possible culprit for Mrs Reeser's demise. And hers is not the only case. According to an article in *Fate* (April 1961) by the Reverend Winogene Savage, a friend's brother awoke one morning to his wife's screams. Rushing to their living room he found her on the floor, ablaze, with a strange fireball hovering over her blackened form. With the help of neighbours and several buckets of water the flames were put out; but the lady later died, and her husband suffered burns from his ministrations. Witnesses noted that although the wife's clothes had been burnt off, there was no scorching on the rug where she had collapsed, and no other sign of fire damage in the room.

Death from natural causes

Maxwell Cade and Delphine Davis include this account in their 1969 study of ball lightning, *Taming of the thunderbolts*, and note its similarity to the records of spontaneous human combustion. They review the theories of several physicists who suggest that the huge energies of ball lightning could, in certain circumstances, manifest short radio waves of the kind used in microwave ovens. And they speculate:

> If this theory is correct . . . it is possible for victims to be burned to death, not merely within their clothes, but even within their skin, either by the proximity of a lightning ball or by having a ball form within their body, or just by the action of the intense radiofrequency field which, in the absence of their body, would have formed a lightning ball at that place.

As it is a natural phenomenon, and because ball lightning is notoriously capricious, it is the best candidate so far for the cause of SHC cases, whether ancient or modern. It would also account for the victims being fried from the inside out. Microwave diathermy can heat different materials at different rates, and this may explain the curious phenomenon of selective burning that is associated with SHC.

Not one of these theories can account by

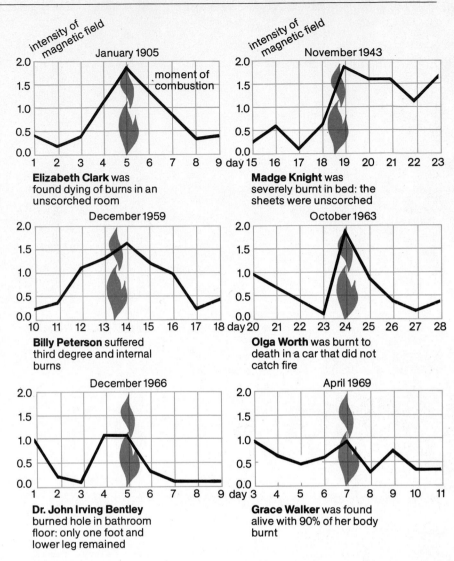

January 1905
moment of combustion
Elizabeth Clark was found dying of burns in an unscorched room

November 1943
Madge Knight was severely burnt in bed: the sheets were unscorched

December 1959
Billy Peterson suffered third degree and internal burns

October 1963
Olga Worth was burnt to death in a car that did not catch fire

December 1966
Dr. John Irving Bentley burned hole in bathroom floor: only one foot and lower leg remained

April 1969
Grace Walker was found alive with 90% of her body burnt

itself for the bizarre varieties of burning that have been authoritatively recorded. The fact that SHC occurs infrequently (if not so rarely as some writers claim) also suggests that it requires special circumstances to come about, and depends on the correct conjunction of many necessary factors. Some we can guess at; others remain unknown. But we can at least offer the following synthesis.

Age and sex seem less important than the victim's psychic and physiological state. We may imagine a lonely, sedentary person, incapacitated by illness or injury, or psychically by despair, fear, depression and perhaps resentment. This incapacity may psychosomatically affect the body and its metabolism, causing an imbalance of phosphagens and erratic behaviour in the body's heat-regulating mechanisms. Normally, this state would pass unnoticed. But imagine that it should happen a few days after intense sunspot activity, with a magnetic storm pushing up the value of the geomagnetic field to abnormal heights for the victim's locality. Now all that is needed is a trigger: a cosmic ray, a natural burst of low-frequency energy, or a lightning ball. And then we have a human bonfire.

The force of the Earth's magnetism is surprisingly uneven. It is unequally distributed around the globe, and fluctuates in intensity (measured in gausses). These six charts show the curious relationship between a high reading on the geomagnetic scale and the incidence of SHC

When fish pour down li

For centuries there have been incidents of fish falling from the sky, the latest as recently as 1975. BOB RICKARD discusses this strange phenomenon, one of the least explicable quirks of nature

ON 16 FEBRUARY 1861 a violent earthquake shook the island of Singapore. For the following six days, rain fell in torrents. Then, on the morning of the 22nd, after a last furious downpour, it stopped. François de Castelnau, a French naturalist staying on the island, reported what happened next to the Academy of Sciences in Paris, later that year.

At 10 a.m. the sun lifted, and from my window I saw a large number of Malays and Chinese filling baskets with fishes which they picked up in the pools of water which covered the ground. On being asked where the fishes came from they answered that they had fallen from the sky. Three days afterwards, when the pools had dried up, we found many dead fishes.

Although de Castelnau did not see the rain of fish himself, he was convinced that they had fallen from the sky. Dr A. D. Bajkov, an American marine scientist, was luckier. On 23 October 1947 he was having breakfast with his wife in a café in Marksville, Louisiana, USA, when shortly after a sudden shower of rain, he noticed fish lying in the streets: 'sunfish, goggle-eyed minnows and black bass up to 9 inches [23 centimetres] long.' More fish were found on rooftops, cold

Right: despite the fact that the phenomenon of fish falling from the sky has been the subject of discussion and eyewitness reports for centuries, no 'natural' explanation has yet been found. This illustration of falling fish comes from a book by Claus Magnus, *Historia de gentibus septentrionalibus* (1555), in which the author discusses falls of fish, frogs and other animals

Far right: one of the most reliably recorded incidents in Britain involved a timber yard worker, John Lewis, of Mountain Ash, Glamorganshire. On 9 February 1859 he was hit by falling fish, as illustrated in Charles Tomlinson's *Raincloud and snowstorm* (1864)

ke rain

and dead, but nevertheless still fit to eat.

On their own, such accounts are not much to go on. Much of the evidence for fish falling from the sky is circumstantial – fish being found, usually after heavy rain, in places and on surfaces where no fish were before. But there are some eyewitness accounts.

One of the best attested cases to have occurred in Britain was at Mountain Ash, Glamorganshire, Wales, in 1859. In a paper published in the *Fortean Times* of Autumn 1979, Robert Schadwald established on the evidence of eyewitness accounts published at the time that it had happened on 9 February 1859. John Lewis, working in a timber yard at Mountain Ash, was startled at 11 a.m. by being suddenly struck by small objects falling out of the sky. One of the objects fell down the back of his neck.

On putting my hand down my neck I was surprised to find they were small fish. By this time I saw that the whole ground was covered with them. I took off my hat, the brim of which was full of them. They were jumping all about . . . The shed [pointing to a large workshop] was covered with them, and the shoots were quite full of them. My mates and I might have gathered bucketsful of them, scraping with our hands . . . There were two showers . . . It was not blowing very hard, but uncommon wet . . . They came down in the rain in 'a body like'.

A similar experience happened some 85 years later to Ron Spencer of Lancashire, while serving with the RAF at Kamilla, India, near the Burmese border. Speaking on BBC Radio 4 in April 1975, after another listener had described his experience of a fish fall, Ron said that he had loved going out into the monsoon rains to wash himself. On one occasion he was standing naked in the middle of this ritual when

Things started to hit me, and looking

round, I could see myriads of small wriggling shapes on the ground and thousands being swept off the roofs, along channels and into the paddy fields. They were small sardine-sized fish. Needless to say, very shortly after the heavy storm none were left. Scavengers had gobbled them up.

No one has yet discovered how often fish falls occur. The records are widely scattered and there is not a full study available that has collected *all* known cases. But it seems that only falls of frogs and toads are more abundant. For example, Dr E. W. Gudger, of the US Museum of Natural History, collected accounts for 40 years, and found only 78 reports spanning 2350 years. Seventeen of these occurred in the USA; 13 in India; 11 in Germany; 9 in Scotland; 7 in Australia; and 5 in England and Canada. But Gilbert Whitley, working from the records in the Australian Museum, lists over 50 fish falls in Australasia alone between 1879 and 1971.

One of the earliest references to a fish fall is to be found in the ancient Greek text the *Deipnosophistai*, compiled at the end of the second century AD by Athenaeus. These fragments, drawn from the records of nearly 800 writers, contain the report:

I know also that it rained fishes. At all events Phoenias, in the second book of his *Eresian magistrates*, says that in the Chersonesus it once rained fishes uninterruptedly for three days and Phylarchus in his fourth book says that the people had often seen it raining fish.

The earliest known case in England happened in Kent in 1666, and was reported in the *Philosophical Transactions* of 1698.

But despite the wealth of authenticated and reliable reports that fish falls have occurred, no one has yet produced a convincing account of *why* they happen. One of the most plausible explanations is that they are caused by tornadoes, waterspouts or whirlwinds lifting water containing fish high up into a cloud mass and carrying them inland.

Other explanations include the suggestion that the phenomenon is caused by fish 'migrating overland'; that fish-eating birds regurgitate or drop their food; that fish are left behind by ponds and streams overflowing; and that fish hibernating in mud are brought to life again by rain. But these do not account for the variety of eyewitness reports, the assortment of species found in the same place, the variety of terrain where fish have been found and the sheer number of fish involved in some cases. And even though there are well-documented cases of whirlwinds and waterspouts transporting fish, this explanation is inadequate to cover *all* cases.

Whirlwinds, tornadoes and waterspouts are very messy. They tend to pick up anything in their way and scatter it in every direction. This conflicts dramatically with the great majority of cases of fish falls. In the

Mountain Ash, for example, witnessed 'two showers, with an interval of ten minutes [between them] and each shower lasted about two minutes, or thereabouts.'

The length of time during which fish have been transported through the air seems, according to the evidence, to vary considerably. In many accounts, the fish are alive and thrashing when found on the ground; in other cases they have been found dead, but fresh and edible. It is difficult to believe that fish could be hurled against the ground and not be killed, but the evidence suggests that even those found dead were not killed by their fall. In his *History of Ceylon*, Sir James Tennant describes fish that were not injured by their fall onto gravel.

More puzzling still are the falls of dead fish. On two occasions in India, at Futtepoor in 1833 and at Allahabad in 1836, the fish that fell from the sky were not only dead, but dried. In the former case, the number of fish that fell was estimated to be between 3000 and 4000, all of one species. It is difficult to imagine how a whirlwind could keep so many fish in the air long enough for them to have dried out. But, despite widespread publicity in the Indian press at the time, no one came forward to report that a whirlwind *had* snatched up a valuable heap of dried fish! Perhaps even more extraordinary is the case from Essen, Germany, in 1896, where a Crucian carp fell out of the sky during a storm, encased in ice. Here, the fish must have been kept aloft by vertical currents long enough to become the nucleus of an egg-sized hailstone.

Sticklebacks from the sky

In the falls of other animals and insects there is a tendency for only one species to descend at any one time. But the evidence available concerning fish falls shows that they can be equally divided between falls of a single species and mixed falls. Up to six different species have been identified in a single fall, lending support to the idea that the phenomenon is caused by a waterspout scooping randomly from seas and lakes.

Falls of single species present many problems. The Mountain Ash fall in Glamorganshire, for example, was found to contain mostly sticklebacks with just a few minnows. Sticklebacks live in freshwater streams and do not congregate in shoals. How was it possible for a whirlwind to have scooped out such a vast quantity of sticklebacks together from a single source and deposit them all in one place? Similar questions apply to other cases of fish falls involving just one species. Another curious feature is the absence of all accompanying debris.

Objects caught up in the currents of a whirlwind might be expected to be hurled out at different times and distances according to their mass, size or shape. Contrary to this expectation, however, fish falls often involve many different sizes of fish. At Feridpoor,

Mountain Ash case, for example, the fall was restricted to an area 80 yards by 12 yards (73 metres by 11 metres). In the Kent case of 1666 it was claimed that the fish were dumped in one particular field and not in any of the surrounding ones. Most falls, in fact, seem to follow this localised pattern. Perhaps the most extreme example of this orderly fall of fish took place south of Calcutta on 20 September 1839. An eyewitness said: 'The most strange thing which ever struck me was that the fish did not fall helter-skelter . . . but in a straight line not more than one cubit [an ancient measurement deriving from the length of the forearm] in breadth.'

Whirlwinds move continuously. There is considerable evidence that fish falls have lasted much longer than the time possible for them to have been caused by a whirlwind. The torrent of many hundreds of sand eels on Hendon, a suburb of Sunderland, north-east England, on 24 August 1918 is a case in point. A. Meek, a marine biologist, reported seeing a fall, that lasted a full 10 minutes and was confined to one small area.

Even if whirlwinds do retrace their path, some fish falls have occurred in such a rapid succession that they could not have been caused by one whirlwind. John Lewis of

Above: one popular theory as to how fish could be transported overland and then 'dropped' from the sky is that water containing quantities of fish is gathered up by tornadoes. This tornado was photographed in Nebraska

India, for example, two species of fish fell in 1830, one larger and heavier than the other. Similarly, fish ranging in length from 6 to 12 inches (15 to 30 centimetres) fell in several gardens in Harlow, Essex, on 12 August 1968, according to next day's newspapers.

Charles Fort, who spent a lifetime collecting accounts of strange phenomena, suggested that fish falls are the result of what he called 'teleportation', a force that can transport objects from place to place without traversing the intervening distance. Such a force, Fort claimed, was once more active than it is now, and survives today as an erratic and feeble semblance of its former self. Through this agency fish are snatched away from a place of abundance to a point in the sky, from which they fall. Sometimes this point is not very high off the ground, which would account for the fact that the fish are often found alive. At other times the point is *very* close to the ground, accounting for the many observations of fish that seem to have appeared on the ground during a rainstorm.

Fort further suggested that fish falls might be the result of a new pond 'vibrating with its need for fish'. There is the case of Major Cox, for example, a well–known writer in England after the First World War. In an article published in the *Daily Mail* on 6 October 1921, Cox reported that the pond at his Sussex home had been drained and scraped of mud. The pond was then left dry for five months before refilling with water in November 1920. The following May, Cox was astonished to find it teeming with tench.

In 1941 the *American Journal of Science* published a story of a farm in Cambridge, Maryland, USA, where work on a new system of drains was halted because of rain. When work resumed, the ditch was found to be full of rainwater and hundreds of perch, of two different species, measuring between 4 and 7 inches (10 to 18 centimetres).

In neither case, however, was there time

for aestivation. Overflows and migrating fish were ruled out because of the distance of both sites from any surrounding water. Fort also ruled out the possibility that the fish fell from the sky since they were found only in the new water. If they had fallen from the sky one would expect there to be some dead fish lying around. But none was found.

Most fish falls occur during heavy rains, so the whirlwind theory seems to be partially acceptable. A look at the range of reported cases, however, shows that a number of falls

Left: another drawing from Claus Magnus' *Historia de gentibus septentrionalibus* (1555) showing fish falling from the sky onto a town

Below: this woodcut showing a man struggling through a torrential shower of rain and fish was based on an 18th century incident in Transylvania

have occurred in cloudless skies and quite independently of any accompanying strong wind. But if teleportation seems too far-fetched – and it is difficult to believe that fish can disappear from one place and reappear in mid-air – what other explanation is there? At present the only rational explanation in terms of known causes seems to be the whirlwind theory. But this, as we have seen, cannot account for all cases. The fish fall remains one of the oddest, and least explicable, quirks of nature – if, indeed, it *is* nature, as we understand it, at work here.

The great escape

When his parachute went up in flames 18,000 feet above Berlin, Flight Sergeant Nicholas Alkemade decided to jump rather than burn to death. The miracle was, as BEALE McIVER reveals, that he survived to tell the tale

FLIGHT SERGEANT Nicholas Alkemade was a little nervous at the thought that this was to be his thirteenth bombing mission over Germany. Just 21 years old, he had the loneliest, most dangerous job in RAF Bomber Command: tail-gunner in a Lancaster. Still, he and the crew of *S for Sugar* had survived so far.

Besides the danger, being tail-gunner in a Lancaster was uncomfortable. There was room enough in that tiny perspex bubble for the gunner, his ammunition and four Browning machine guns. And that was all. Even the parachute had to be stowed outside the turret. At 20,000 feet (6000 metres) it could get very cold indeed – and 24 March 1944 was a chilly spring night.

Little bothered the flight from 115 Squadron as they droned over the German mainland. A little flak above Frankfurt, then Berlin – already lit up by Pathfinder flares and the sharp beams of searchlights trying to ensnare the 300 Allied bombers that had come to pound the beleaguered enemy capital that night. At last, Alkemade heard the magic words: 'Bombs away!' Two tonnes of high explosive and nearly three of incendiaries dropped away. At once the pilot, Jack Newman, turned the big plane toward home and safety.

There was one massive explosion. Then cannon shells tearing down the fuselage towards Alkemade. Two ripped through his turret, shattering the perspex. Splinters dug into him. Then he saw the attacker: a lone Junkers 88, closing in now to finish off the

Top left: an Avro Lancaster bomber. Capable in some versions of carrying 10 tonnes of bombs, it was used against German industry as well as in incendiary raids on enemy cities – like the one Sgt Alkemade flew in March 1944

Top right: the versatile Junkers 88 was adapted to many combat roles. A night fighter version crippled Alkemade's *S for Sugar* – and brought about a miracle

Above: Nicholas Alkemade, alive and well despite several close encounters with death

wounded bomber. Alkemade aimed and fired, his tracer arcing toward the enemy, now only 50 yards (45 metres) distant. The Junker's port engine exploded and it dipped away, doomed. Alkemade was elated.

Not for long. Flames were already leaping past the remains of his turret. In a moment Jack Newman's voice came over the intercom: 'You'll have to jump for it. Bail out. Bail out.' Unfortunately, that, for Alkemade, meant retrieving his parachute from its rack behind him – somewhere amid those tongues of fire. He shoved open the doors into the fuselage momentarily and gaped at the blaze within. But this was his only hope. He tried again, spotted the parachute – then watched in horror as it disintegrated in flames.

'My stomach seemed to drop out of my body,' he said. 'I now knew that I was going to die. I said to myself, "You've had your lot."'

But not, he decided, by being burnt to death. 'Better a quick, clean death than frying.' Nicholas Alkemade was going to jump. Tearing off his already melting oxygen mask, he managed to manoeuvre the turret so that the hole faced toward the rear again. Then he somersaulted backwards into space.

Sheer relief at once replaced the terror. Alkemade felt perfectly calm. As he later put it: 'It was perfectly quiet and cool, like resting on a cloud . . . as though I was lowered onto a super-soft mattress. There was no sensation of falling. . . . I thought, well, if this is dying, it's not so bad.'

Indeed he felt so peaceful that he was able to calculate that from 18,000 feet (5500 metres) it would take him 90 seconds to hit the ground. And he had been looking forward to his next leave in a week's time. Now he wouldn't be seeing his girlfriend Pearl. Lying on his back in the air, he gazed at the

stars and thought how foolish Man's struggles seemed. Then he passed out.

Alkemade couldn't understand why he felt so cold. He was supposed to be dead. He opened an eye. A star shone through the fir trees above him. He dug out his cigarette case and lighter, suddenly desperate for a smoke, then checked the time. It was 3.10 a.m. and he had been unconscious for three hours. 'Jesus Christ,' he said out loud. 'I'm alive.'

Somehow, the trees had broken his fall. Eighteen inches (45 centimetres) of snow made a final cushion. He had dropped over 3 miles (5 kilometres) out of the sky and lived to tell the tale. Not only that – he was hardly damaged at all. Some burns, a badly twisted right knee, but everything else seemed to work. He couldn't walk, and then began to worry about exposure. 'The prospect of being a POW didn't seem so bad. I wanted to be found.'

Members of the local *Volkssturm* heard the blasts from his regulation whistle, and found him still smoking his cigarette. When they picked him up he fainted. And then the problems began.

He was taken to hospital, and tried to explain what had happened to a doctor. 'Nix parachute,' he announced. The doctor smiled mirthlessly and tapped his head gently. Obviously Alkemade was mad. At Dalag Luft POW camp near Frankfurt it was no better. Alkemade suffered three interrogations and solitary confinement for sticking to his unbelievable story. He was clearly lying, and just as clearly he was really a spy.

But Alkemade heard that a Lancaster had been reported crashing on the night of 24 March near where he was found. Perhaps it was *S for Sugar*. And perhaps the remains of his parachute could be found in the wreck. Leutnant Hans Feidal of the Luftwaffe was eventually persuaded to look into the story. Sure enough, the harness of the tail-gunner's

parachute was there, and was brought back. Alkemade tried it on. The snaphooks and lift webbing were still tied down with thread – and would have broken had the parachute been opened. Then the Germans found the scorched handle of the ripcord in the wreckage. The camp commandant could only pronounce Alkemade's escape a miracle.

His fellow prisoners later presented him with the flyleaf of a Bible. On it was written:

DALAG LUFT

It has been investigated and corroborated by the German authorities that the claim made by Sergeant Alkemade 1431537 RAF, is true in all respects, namely that he made a descent from 18,000 feet without parachute and made a safe landing without injury, his parachute having been on fire in the aircraft. He landed in deep snow among fir trees.

Corroboration witnessed by:

Flt Lt H. J. Moore, Senior British Officer.

Flt Sgt R. R. Lamb 1339582.

Flt Sgt T. A. Jones 411 Senior British NCO. Date 25.4.44.

Nicholas Alkemade survived his thirteenth bombing mission, against all the odds. And he continued to live a charmed life. He worked in a chemical factory in his home town of Loughborough after the war. Once a 224-pound (100-kilogram) steel girder fell on him. He was hauled out for dead, but walked away with a bruised scalp. On another occasion he was drenched with sulphuric acid. He had an electric shock that threw him into a hole where he lay breathing chlorine gas for a quarter of an hour, and lived to tell that tale as well. Someone, somewhere, is looking after Nicholas Alkemade.

Below: the cramped quarters of a Lancaster's tail gun bubble. A rear gunner was known in the RAF as 'arse-end Charlie' – an attempt at humour that failed to disguise the high mortality rate that went with the job

Below right: the airman's view of an incendiary raid on a sleeping German city. These attacks were intended to demoralise the civilian population. Though very destructive, they failed in their psychological objective

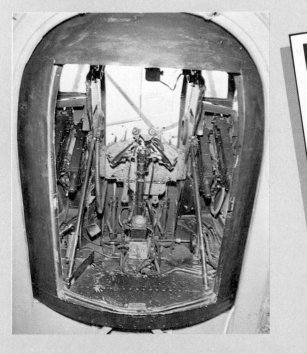

Index